Client Badassery Secrets

How Copywriters Can Earn MORE, Run a Thriving Freelance Business, and Cut Out the Client Bullsh*t

Kim Krause Schwalm

Foreword by
Marcella Allison

Get Dangerously Good Publishing

Contents

First Printing: 2023

ISBN: 979-8-9889590-0-7

Download the Client Badassery Secrets Tool Kit for FREE

As a way to thank you for reading my book, I'd like to give you two valuable companion tools to use as you apply your newfound client badassery: my *Client Badassery Secrets Client Screening Questionnaire* and my *Client Badassery Secrets Sales Call Script*… absolutely FREE.

Go to toolkit.clientbadasserysecrets.com to claim yours now!

Praise

for Kim Krause Schwalm and her Client Badassery Secrets

"If you aspire to be rich and famous as a freelance copywriter, this book is for you. Kim is a rock star in copywriting circles, and this is her 'how-to' guide of how to succeed as a highly-paid freelancer. She holds nothing back.

"For example, she reveals how to leverage the power of referrals to fill up your schedule with good clients and build a thriving freelance business. She'll tell you how to avoid the nightmare clients who will take advantage of you and give you untold grief. She shares negotiating tactics for getting paid more money, and how to raise your rates and have clients say 'yes.'

"In her own career, Kim has sat on both sides of the table— as both a client who hires freelancers and then as a successful freelancer herself. So she knows the strategies and tactics that work well to help you and your clients thrive. It's one of the best investments you'll ever make in your career."

— *Gary Bencivenga, Business Owner and Retired Direct Response Copywriter*

"Want to flourish as a copywriter? Read this book. *Why?* Irving Wunderman, brother of Lester, who coined the phrase Direct Marketing, said the big question when writing copy is, 'To whom are you offering what ultimate benefit?' The big question any writer should ask is, 'How can I make more money?' Kim's book tells you."

— *Drayton Bird, Author,* Commonsense Direct Marketing

"I've known and worked with Kim for more than 3 decades. We traded our client 'war stories' with each other in our early days of freelance copywriting. If there's anyone you can trust who's handled just about every type of nightmare client and situation, it's Kim.

"That's why you can trust her to help YOU steer clear of them and handle these situations like a pro. Plus Kim shows you how to build your freelance biz and help your income soar to new heights!

"Her book is a MUST HAVE."

— *Carline Anglade-Cole, Award-Winning Copywriter & Author*

"This book will help you steer clear of nightmare clients, including 7 types Kim identifies in hilariously accurate detail. She also lays out how to attract the dream ones, and confidently charge higher fees plus negotiate royalty deals— something I never did as a copywriter. I retired my client services, but who knows... If I'd had the info in Kim's book 10 or 15 years ago, I may have hit my first million way sooner!"

— *Laura Belgray, Author,* Tough Titties, *and Founder,* TalkingShrimp.com

"Finally, a book with the balls to tell it like it is about clients and negotiations. Can I get an amen? This book ain't just overdue, it's criminally late! Kim talks about scrounging up the ones who pay well, getting every hard-earned dollar you deserve from them, and beefing up your confidence. You'll be a negotiation ninja after reading this puppy. Best of all, with *Client Badassery Secrets*, you'll step up your game, *and* your paycheck."

— *Lorrie "Lo" Morgan, Copywriting Mentor, RedHotCopy.com*

"I've always been amazed at how easily Kim Krause Schwalm can not only get high-class clients in her sleep, but also helps her coaching clients get booked out months in advance even when they couldn't get so much as a return phone call before.

If I was seeking clients, Kim is the first person I'd consult with on the subject. She did it during far more hostile conditions than copywriters have today. And has a proven track record of helping others do the same."

— *Ben Settle, Founder and Author, BenSettle.com*

"You can be the most gifted copywriter on the planet, but without clients—no one will benefit from your brilliance. Which is why if you want to get clients, you must listen to Kim Krause Schwalm. Kim's decades of real-world experience being an A-list copywriter with some of the biggest companies in the world shine through in her new book *Client Badassery Secrets*.

"Read it today!"

— *Ryan Lee, Founder, Author, RyanLee.com*

"You need to be a 'badass' to use 'badassery' in the title of a book... and there is not a more qualified badass than Kim Krause Schwalm to pull it off. She is a badass of epic proportions because she has excelled working on both sides of the desk in the most competitive marketplaces in direct response marketing.

"First as a top marketer at one of the most dynamic publishing companies in the 1990's (Phillips Publishing), hiring every top copywriter in the industry during her stint there, working and learning alongside the best-of-the-best.

"And then, when she ventured out as a copywriter on her own, she had seen it all... 'ready for action' would be a huge understatement... and she carved out a vision and version of what it takes to be a world class copywriter that few can match... and now she is ready to share.

"This book is the documentation of that vision and version. *Client Badassery Secrets* is the essential roadmap to success as a freelance copywriter—from nailing down your dream clients... to negotiating from a place of respect (which she earned and has the scars to prove it) ... to spilling the beans on the lies that clients tell copywriters (from her unique perspective as a client and a copywriter) ... and so much more.

"There's also so much value here that is not just for copywriters... on building a business you love, being self-assured and confident... and creating your unfair advantage by implementing Kim's hard-won techniques for working with people you love... because they love you. That's badass."

— *Brian Kurtz, Titans Marketing, Author of*
Overdeliver: Build a Business for a Lifetime Playing
the Long Game in Direct Response Marketing *and*
The Advertising Solution

"Overwhelming in its completeness, this book somehow condenses Kim's decades of experience—hard-earned learnings from hundreds of successful promos and hundreds of millions in sales—into 14 effortlessly readable chapters.

"An instant, bingeable classic that should be required reading for anyone interested in making a living as a copywriter."

— *Eddie Shleyner, Founder, VeryGoodCopy.com*

"*Client Badassery Secrets* belongs in the hands of every freelancer. Kim has navigated a brilliant career, and the respect of an entire industry, by making bold choices and leading with quality work.

"In this book, she is teaching from the scars that produce the wisdom that only very few have. I only wish it had been around when I started."

— *Kevin Rogers, Founder, CopyChief.com*

"If you're tired of being burned by bum clients who don't want to pay you what you're worth, do the dreaded 'scope creep' every chance they get, and sap whatever confidence you can muster up by trying to bend you to their will, Kim is your girl.

"Her *Client Badassery Secrets* book is packed with the confidence-boosting, real life big-sister/trusted mentor advice you can only get from a seasoned A-list copywriter who's successfully freelanced for more than 25 years... plus spent time on the client side. She's truly seen it all, and doesn't hold back on anything. My advice? Read every word, soak up every lesson and tactic, then put them to work and profit!"

— *Kira Hug, Co-Founder, The Copywriter Club*

"No matter what level you are at as a copywriter, do yourself a huge favor by following the advice Kim Krause Schwalm dishes out in Chapter 6 on negotiating fees.

"Kim flat out exposes the real-world truth which keeps copywriters from leveling up and explains how to get unstuck so you can fast track your way to the top of the freelance copywriting world."

— *Bond Halbert, Direct Marketing Consultant, Author &*
Copywriting Mentor

"The difference between those who succeed and those who don't? Badassery—and Kim has plenty of it.

"What truly makes Kim a badass when it comes to client acquisition is that she understands what it means to own your own value and set the boundaries for success.

"Instead of waiting for what you want, Kim will show you how carve your own success path, avoid client pitfalls and stand in your own power. If you want to have a successful career as a freelancer, Kim combines the step-by-step process with incredible mindset strategies to move forward!

"I highly recommend this book."

— *Linda Perry, Mindset Coach & Strategist*

"A collection of hard-won wisdom for dealing with clients, from one of the most experienced copywriters in the game. Kim has packed some excellent advice into this book—and probably could charge a lot more money for it.

"An excellent resource for any new copywriter!"

— *Daniel Throssell, PersuasivePage.com*

"Believe it or not, it's at least as hard to become a successful copywriter, freelance or staff, as it is to learn the skill of copywriting at a high level. The case can be made that it's even harder.

"Top gun copywriter Kim Krause Schwalm has changed all that. In this book, she pulls back the curtain on some of the most closely-guarded secrets in the business: how to attract and retain high-paying copywriting clients, get paid, and hold on to your sanity in the process.

"There's never been such a detailed, practical, real-world guide on how to navigate the treacherous terrain of selling copy. Kim's packaged her priceless know-how in book form, but the information is so valuable it could easily have been delivered as an uber-expensive seminar and still would be a great value!"

— *Ken McCarthy, Internet Pioneer and Founder of the System Seminar, KenMcCarthy.com*

"Where was this book when I needed it most? Actually, who am I kidding… I still need this book! In fact, anyone who calls themselves a copywriter or freelancer does too. *Client Badassery Secrets* is filled with Kim's extensive experience and expertise in client acquisition and management.

"This book is written by a woman who has had to work hard for everything she has and all she has achieved. This alone makes the book a must-read for anyone pursuing long-lasting success as a copywriter. Kim's straightforward and practical advice will save the sanity of those who read it and, most importantly, heed it."

— *Pauline Longdon, Chief Copywriter, TheCopyAlchemist.com*

"Kim's new book reveals countless client-getting secrets for copywriters at every stage of the journey. It's a secret weapon for navigating the shark-infested waters of working with big-time clients.

"It'll be very hard not to get a sizeable ROI following the advice in this book."

— Chris Orzechowski, Top Email Copywriter and Founder,
Orzy Media

"This book has more valuable client-getting tactics than most $997 courses. Anyone struggling with getting clients, or running a freelancing business should read this!"

— Justin Goff, Entrepreneur, Email Marketer, and Mentor,
JustinGoff.com

"If you want a predictable stream of high-quality, high-paying and no-stress clients—this book is the only one you need to devour. The lessons, strategies, and tactics are decades in the making and don't fall prey to the latest shiny object you're getting pitched daily.

"Don't read anything else. Don't listen to anyone else. Just do what Kim tells you.

"I'm amazed she's giving away so much, for so little. This stuff works—whether you're new or experienced. I feel bad for all the other copywriting gurus and charlatans.

"Actually, I don't. They deserve to fail and become broke, busted, and disgusted. Read this book. Do the things. Make a crap ton of money."

— Samuel Woods, Investor, AI Expert, Copywriter
SamuelJWoods.com

"Wanna make a living as a freelance copywriter? Easy. Just do these two things. First, master the craft. Second, become a master not just at getting clients but also at keeping them, getting the best deals out of them, and making sure they plug you into the most lucrative projects around.

"Because when it comes to making BIG money as a freelancer, those things are just as important as your copywriting skill. Maybe even more so. Kim's new book handles that part of the equation for you. The guidance it contains could easily be worth 10s of thousands, even 100s of thousands in added annual income. Read it now!"

— *Dan Ferrari, Top Freelance Copywriter,*
FerrariMedia.com

"In discovering Kim's work, you've just hit the copywriting client-getting jackpot.

"First, she's been there, done that, and succeeded with the A-list of marketing clients, who only retain the very best copywriters.

"Second, she's enthusiastically willing to tell all, and share her greatest secrets to this success.

"Third, she is also wildly effective at teaching her skill, which is rare among those with skills you truly want and need to learn.

"Fourth, her content writing here and elsewhere is as compelling as her copy, which makes this a wonderful read. And fifth, she actually cares about your success, not just getting your money.

"Go all-in on learning from Kim—you will not regret it."

— *Roy Furr, Direct Response Copywriter & Copy Chief*

"How to handle your copywriting business is a topic I've been obsessed with since I started copywriting way back in 2009. It felt like a few pros had it figured out. They knew all the secrets and the rest of us had to put in our time and figure it out.

"And that meant dealing with low-paying, demanding clients that sucked up all my time and energy and didn't even reward me for the pleasure.

"Then I met Kim.

"The first day we met she leaned in during dinner and said, 'I want to help you. Anything you need, reach out.' And I took her up on that!

"She helped me negotiate my first royalty deal with one of the 'big guys' of direct response and warned me about a few landmines I might encounter along the way. She knew this particular client and was happy to help me skip some of the painful learning curve.

"Now, she's put all that elusive pro knowledge into this incredible resource. It's an absolute must-read for anyone starting out in copy (or any freelancing really)... and offers hard-earned tips and tricks for those of us that have been in the business awhile.

"Copywriting is a career centered around people and relationships. Crafting a successful copywriting career is so much more than writing words that sell. It's dealing with clients, figuring out what to charge, and understanding how to manage tricky situations. And there's two ways to master these skills: mess it up over years or read this book cover-to-cover."

— *Abbey Woodcock, Founder, Oneida Freelance Co-op*

"*Client Badassery Secrets* by Kim Krause Schwalm is a must-read for every freelance copywriter looking to elevate their craft and master the art of negotiation.

"Honestly, it's like getting the lowdown over coffee with one of the best in the biz, with advice and insights only years on the front lines can teach. Kim doesn't mince words, serving up those hard truths we all need to swallow if we're serious about our craft. And pay attention, because you're also witnessing the finesse of a master copywriter—the subheadings are rich with lessons in their own right.

"This isn't just a book—it's a real-world masterclass from a seasoned pro, and your opportunity to shortcut your way to success."

— *Belinda Weaver, Copy Coach and Mentor, Copywrite Matters*

"This book is a rare opportunity to absorb the hard-won lessons about what it really takes to have a thriving freelance copywriting career for over 3 decades.

"From 'hard' skills like negotiating higher fees and drafting contract terms to protect yourself... to "softer" skills like setting boundaries and positioning yourself as an authority... this book has it all.

"Which means now the rest of us also have the opportunity to enjoy long and successful careers as freelance copywriters.

"And that's why I recommend *Client Badassery Secrets* to any freelance copywriter who wants to run a more profitable and less stressful business."

— *Brian Speronello, Copywriter & Founder of FreelanceLikeAPro.com*

"Kim's *Client Badassery Secrets* is a fantastic resource for any freelance copywriter looking to succeed. It's got some exceptional lessons on everything from ensuring clients don't walk all over you to negotiating better deals. There are lessons in this book for copywriters of all levels. It's a crazy amount of wisdom for such a quick, engaging read that you'll sail right through. If you're a copywriter, it could end up being the best money you've spent!"

— *Jon Buchan, Founder, Charm Offensive*

"I laughed out loud when I read 'Big Client Lie #2: That's the final launch plan.' Yeah, I've been there, too and it's tough. Changing upsells, rewriting the bonuses, or even changing the whole damn offer is a painful and common occurrence when working with clients. When I was young in my marketing career, I would bend and fold to my client's demands, sacrificing my sleep, sanity and profit just to ensure they were happy. But as Kim points out, the client does not need a contortionist. They need an expert, who has boundaries, and delivers high-quality copy on-time.

"It doesn't matter how great your copy is if you allow yourself to get railroaded by clients. And Chapter 8 shares an 'Always Be...' commandment that only foolish copywriters will choose to ignore. This whole book is written to the copywriter who wants to take their career seriously, provide for their family, reduce their downside and create ways to be paid asymmetrically for their value. It should be a required reading, especially if you're not allergic to humor. What Kim has written is worthy of space on your shelf, squeezed between Halbert, Schwartz, Zinsser, and Cialdini."

— *Casey Stanton, #1 Wall Street Journal Bestselling Author of* The Fractional CMO Method

"In an industry still heavily dominated by men, Kim Krause Schwalm continues to make a name for herself as one of the most successful women.

"How did she make it to the top? By writing great copy, of course... but also by knowing how to seek out and land clients, negotiate with them, and relate to them.

"Kim has always run her business like a business, and if you want to do the same, then you'll find tons of value packed into this fast-paced read. Get ready for page after page of Kim's tips, wins, and philosophies developed after more than 25 years in the trenches... and a few cringeworthy stories, too.

"This is a book I know I'll return to again (and again)."

— *Candice Lazar, Direct Response Marketer and Launch Specialist*

"I've been friends with Kim Schwalm for years, ever since we had steak and wine with a group of friends after a marketing conference in Orlando.

"In the copywriting world, Kim is the cream of the crop—a certified A-lister. I've seen her work for the top clients, beat 'unbeatable' controls, and climb to the top of super-competitive niches. On top of that, she's a pleasure to be around and shoot the wind with. I love her teaching style, and I've heard from a slew of copywriters that she's one of the best coaches and mentors around.

"If you're a copywriter interested in enjoying a long, successful career with a lot of big royalty checks, I definitely recommend you follow Kim and learn whatever you can from her... you'll be glad you did."

— *Ning Li, A-List Copywriter and Copy Chief at PaleoHacks*

"If you want to run a successful copywriting business, learning to write copy is just the first step. Kim Krause Schwalm can teach you to write great copy. But Kim also knows copywriting is a business. You have to learn how to find great clients, negotiate airtight deals with fair terms, and manage your business relationships with a no-BS, badass approach.

"This book covers all that and more. Because it focuses on the business of copywriting, this book will—as its subtitle promises—empower you to earn more and eliminate bullsh*t from your life. (Hello, mutually-beneficial relationships with lucrative dream clients; bye-bye, soul-sucking, scope-creeping gigs with jerk clients).

"This is a playbook that every copywriter should read and master. Great for new copywriters who want to launch a solid business. Equally great for experienced copywriters who want to plug leaks, not repeat the same mistakes again, and stand out as the go-to copywriter in their niche. 5 ☆!"

— *Tom Ruwitch, Founder, StorypowerMarketing.com*

"There are very few books on client-wrangling that I'd ever recommend… but this is the exception. Because while most are based on a single technique that doesn't apply across the board, Kim gives the honest truth about what actually works at any level. If you're going to learn this (and you absolutely should) skip the trial-and-error and go straight to the best – a veteran writer who has paved the path for us all and built a business on boundaries, morals, and a buttload of badassery. You may not like everything Kim has to say about client management—and if you're a client, you definitely won't… but that doesn't mean she's wrong!"

— *Justin Blackman, Brand Voice Expert,*
BrandVoiceAcademy.com

"If you are a copywriter who wants better clients, more money, and boundless freedom, then this book is for you. Not only does this book focus on how to attract quality clients as a freelance copywriter (and avoid the tire kickers), it will also show you how to negotiate your fees and retainers like a boss. No more freelance feast and famine! I have been a successful fractional CMO and Copy Chief for over 10 years and I know that the secret to long-term freelance success is working with clients who value your work from the get-go.

"Kim's book, *Client Badassery Secrets*, is packed with hard-won client-getting (and keeping) tricks from one of the strongest and most successful women in the biz. Learn from her today and future-proof your freelance business for tomorrow."

— *Misty Santos, CEO, Disgraceful Marketing*

"Eye-opening insights from one of the world's best copywriters.... the three 'catbird seat' tips are worth the price of admission alone! Any copywriter who uses the secrets in this book to their advantage will be able to handle themselves like a seasoned pro."

— *Cain Smith, Founder, HookLineConversion.com*

"Kim's book had me from the first chapter... when you go into business for yourself as a freelancer, you just became a marketer of your services, as well. You won't have any work if you don't market yourself. Kim's proven points from being a successful, in-the-trenches, always-in-demand freelance writer will put you on the path to consistently generating income. She has lived it and knows what works (and doesn't work). I highly recommend freelancers at any level seeking a consistent income get this book!"

— *Lisa Rangel, CEO, Chameleon Resumes*

"Instead of writing some general 'this is a GREAT book!' endorsement, I want to highlight one specific section that connects with me personally; a section called 'Build a thriving freelance business... by going in-house?' Why does this relate to me? Well, the simple 'secret' inside this subchapter is what gave me my big break in my early years of copywriting.

"(And for that matter, it was at Kim's *Copywriting Velocity* event where this big break came from. So that's DOUBLY the reason to pay attention to Kim's teachings!)

"It's the reason I've gone from 'nobody' to 'top tier earner'; now making $20k+ per month for multiple years. Funny thing is, it's not just me... many of my close friends (also highly-paid writers) followed this same path to success. I consider it a 'shortcut' for the newer writer; a 'shortcut' I've personally seen work time and time again for up-and-coming writers struggling to get a foothold in the industry.

"I highly suggest you get this book, read it through, and pay mind to this section, specifically."

— *Jerrod Harlan, Head of Email, ClickFunnels*

"Whether you're just getting started in marketing or copywriting, or a seasoned pro, this juicy resource is sure to provide all the details you need for success in every situation.

"The stories and wide-open shares are delightful and jam-packed with fresh solutions. From imposter syndrome to failing, and knowing how to properly push forward toward success... Kim spells it all out.

"A must-read for our entire industry."

— *Lori Haller, Designing Response*

"As a seasoned freelance marketer, I am no stranger to the trials, tribulations, and triumphs of navigating the unpredictable yet rewarding world of freelancing. *Client Badassery Secrets* provides an insightful new perspective that has changed how I approach my business.

"This book serves as an empowering manual that redefines the rules of freelancing, turning challenges into stepping stones towards success.

"Kim's narrative reminds me that I'm not just a freelancer, but a badass freelancer ready to conquer any obstacle that comes my way."

— *Ted Prodromou, YourLinkedInCoach.com*

"Kim isn't just one of the world's top copywriters, she's also an incredible business coach.

"This book will help you level up your pitching and negotiating skills and improve your client management systems—so you can grow a lucrative AND enjoyable freelance business."

— *Rachael Pilcher, B2B SaaS Copywriter*

"Kim is one of the boldest and most assertive copywriters I know. If you want to learn how to take control of your career and negotiate deals like a true pro—this book gives you a clear blueprint for success."

— *Rachel Mazza, Business Consultant, Mazza Media and CMO, Copy Chief*

"Kim's *Client Badassery Secrets* is THE book I wish I had when I got started as a freelance copywriter. It's exactly what beginner freelance copywriters need to eliminate nightmare clients from their life for good, get paid what they're worth, and gain unshakable confidence when it comes to client work. Go get yourself a copy now because it's gonna change your life!"

— *Csaba Borzási, Founder, Game of Conversions*

"I'm guessing I'm older than many of the other readers of this book, but I'm still learning this business. I'm also not a direct response copywriter nor do I have any desire to be one. But I wish there was an AI out there somewhere that would enable me to do download the insights in this book directly into my brain. It's pretty much the definitive guide to setting up as a freelance copywriter and getting better at your trade. And it's a quick read, too!"

— *Mike Garner, Author,* Stories That Matter

"Just got done reading *Client Badassery Secrets* and I'm mad. Kim, where were you (and this awesome advice) when I was first getting started in copywriting?! You would have saved me a whole lot of hassle, not to mention shaved years off my learning curve! I probably would have felt better about myself too... because back then I didn't understand what you so eloquently put into words: even A-list copywriters bomb. I had to learn through a lot of trial and error, only to discover that copy skills and business skills were BOTH critical to my freelance success.

"This book is an excellent primer on getting clients, spotting (and dodging) red flags, figuring out how to negotiate from a place of strength (even when you're not an A-lister), and so much more. If you're a copywriter looking to become a freelancer, grab it now."

— *Angie Colee, Business Coach & Host,* Permission to Kick Ass *podcast*

"This book is ladened with stellar ways to create a lucrative copywriting business, and you can't learn this from a better mentor: Kim Schwalm walks her talk.

"Her no-nonsense writing style helps you cut through the fluff and get what you need to take the next steps.

"The networking advice to attend paid events, alone, is worth more than 500 times the cost of this book—at least.

"You'll also find ways to weed out problem clients and attract your dream ones, while charging the top-tier rates your writing is worth."

— *Cindy Childress, The Expert's Ghostwriter®*

"When it comes to direct response copy, Kim Schwalm is a true A-lister.

"That's why we've interviewed her on our podcast to bust myths and share the writing and business habits that make an A-lister. It's why we've asked her to speak at the very first Copywriter Club IRL event, to share her control-beating secrets (and then invited her back a second time to share how she lands project after project with her clients). It's why she's a favorite for Q&As in our Copywriter Think Tank mastermind.

"And it's why I recommended her writing program (and this book) to my own daughter when she was thinking about becoming a copywriter.

"I guess that's a long way of saying she's among the go-to copywriters I trust. And you can trust what she has to say, too."

— *Rob Marsh, Co-Founder, The Copywriter Club*

"The secrets shared in this book are undoubtedly badass. Sure, it'll teach you how to close more clients... But what most gurus don't tell you is that not all clients are created equal — some require FAR more stress than others. Kim masterfully lays out the good, bad, and ugly truths of the copywriting business, and how you can enjoy your work life more than ever WHILE closing as many clients as you please."

— Troy Ericson, CEO, Email Paramedic and Owner, Copywriting.org

"Everyone talks about how to become a better copywriter. Almost nobody talks about the business of being a copywriter. Kim's done a great job showing the good, the bad, and the ugly of being a freelance copywriter and how to navigate the nuances one can only get through years of wisdom and experience. I wish I'd read this book when I first started out."

— Ed Reay, Founder of CopyRecruitment.com and CopyJobBoard.com

"Kim is the real deal when it comes to copywriting: she's an OG control-beater, a whip-smart woman who built herself a new table in a male-dominated sphere, and a phenomenal coach and mentor. Her no-BS approach to both the art and strategy of copywriting, along with the business of maintaining a successful career in the sphere for the long haul, is second to none. There's no one out there quite like her.

"You're gonna wanna read this book!"

— Hillary Weiss Presswood, Creative Director and Positioning Coach for Creatives

Foreword

When I first started out as a copywriter, there were very few women in direct response advertising. At the time, I was being mentored by some of the smartest and best men in the business. But I was struggling.

I felt like a fish out of water trying to figure out how to breathe in this strange new world. I was losing my confidence in myself and my ability to succeed. I was seriously considering giving up.

Then, I discovered Kim Krause Schwalm.

At the time, Kim was one of the very few female copywriters working at the top of her game. She had already racked up an impressive track record of writing winning copy for a wide range of respected publishers, leading supplement companies, and *New York Times* best-selling authors.

I was in awe of her copywriting skills, but more than anything, I admired her hustle and her confidence.

Now I'm not talking about the kind of false bravado and puffery you see everywhere online today...

I'm talking about the confidence that comes from having spent more than 13 years in various marketing positions—from marketing director to brand manager to publisher, before she ever tried her hand at freelance copywriting.

I'm talking about the confidence that comes from having helped launch and run the successful Healthy Directions supplement business, growing it to the equivalent of more than $40 million in sales in today's dollars within its first 3 years.

I'm talking about the bragging rights that come from having beaten many of the top men in the industry in head-to-head tests.

In short, by the time I met her, Kim had already achieved what I only dreamed about achieving someday. Not only that, but she had done it "dancing backwards in high heels" as the saying goes.

The first time I met Kim in person, I was attending a conference where Kim was speaking, and I decided to corner her in the bar. She was sitting on one of the couches at the end of the bar drinking her glass of Pinot Noir when I walked over, pulled up a chair, and asked if I could talk with her.

Kim very graciously said yes, and that's how I found myself pouring out my struggles as a "copy cub" for a legendary male copywriter in the industry.

I confessed that I was under a ton of stress personally, with a family member suffering from mental illness and addiction. I explained that I was barely surviving on the money I earned as a copy cub and I needed to "bring home the bacon."

Then I took a huge swig of my drink and confessed, "I just don't think I have what it takes to succeed in this business. I'm thinking of quitting."

Kim slammed her glass down on the table so hard I was surprised it didn't shatter and said, "Absolutely. Not."

She then proceeded to give me the pep talk to end all pep talks.

She reminded me that I had already racked up multiple successful promos in the highly competitive financial and health niches.

She commiserated with what it's like to be critically "mentored to death" by some of the best in the business. Then she went on to point out that all that mentoring was worth hundreds of thousands of dollars in future royalties if I could just stick with it.

Finally, as a mother and a wife, she knew firsthand what it was like to try to juggle both family and work. She knew what it was like to feel like you were failing at both. And she wasn't having any of my self-flagellation.

She reminded me that I had managed to get my son the help he needed, built a loving and supportive home for our children, and continued to be there for my husband and our family. She told me, "You are the ultimate mama bear."

Then she went on to systematically show me how to better negotiate and handle my relationships with my mentors and my clients in detail.

She showed me how to set better boundaries and to ask for what I needed.

She reminded me that I was not a victim and that I could choose to put myself in the driver's seat.

And. I. Did.

It's no exaggeration to say that I would not have had the incredibly successful career I have today as a multi-six figure copywriter with controls that have generated over $200 million in sales if it wasn't for that infamous pep talk.

I was curled up on top of the proverbial "ledge" that night and about ready to jump... to GIVE UP on myself and my dreams... and Kim mentored me off that ledge like a badass.

Now you can have the same opportunity I had. Pour yourself a glass of wine or your favorite sparkling beverage. Get comfy on your couch. Imagine Kim sitting across from you, a nice glass of Pinot Noir in her hand, giving you the pep talk and wisdom of a lifetime.

Client Badassery Secrets is the advice that Kim shared with me that night, but it's so much more. It's the confidence you need to grab the brass ring and achieve your dreams.

Read it. Follow her advice to the letter.

Then, once you, too, have achieved the level of success that Kim and I have been fortunate enough to experience, turn around and pay it forward—just as Kim has done for you in this book.

Kim's mentored dozens of copywriters, marketers, and business owners, including some of today's hottest rising superstars. Now she's mentoring YOU with *Client Badassery Secrets*.

Step away from that ledge. Dive in, take notes, and put her wisdom to work for you today.

Marcella Allison
Successful A-List Copywriter, Mentor, and Copy Chief... Founder of the Mentoress Collective... and Author of the bestselling book, *Why Didn't Anybody Tell Me This Sh*t Before?*

*For all the copywriters and business owners
I've trained or mentored…*

*for all the great clients I've worked with…
and for all the crappy ones, too…*

(thanks for the lessons so I can share them with others!)

Introduction

How I discovered the awesome power of "badassery" to get what I want

I'll never forget the time when I was 14, and we were living in suburban Dayton, Ohio. It was getting late, and I was hungry for dinner.

I went to ask my mom when dinner would be ready.

She told me, "It's ready now. I'm just waiting for Billy's friend Johnny to leave."

"Billy" was my 12-year-old younger brother.

So I decided to "handle it" rather than wait around and be hungry.

I marched down to my brother's room and saw him and Johnny hanging out.

And I told Johnny, "You have to leave now. We're getting ready to eat dinner."

Johnny left, just like that.

I then marched back to the kitchen and told my mom, "Johnny left. Let's eat!"

I was always direct and to the point.

Feelings? Sorry, get over it… *you're holding up dinner, dude!*

As the oldest, I recognized early on the power I held within the family, at least over my younger brothers.

I started running the old 'hood at an early age, stalking the suburban sidewalks, and making my younger brother cry (until the youngest one came along).

Maybe it was all those hours we spent watching *Mutual of Omaha's Wild Kingdom* on the family room TV.

Understanding that predators have a certain power over prey… but prey can be wily and outsmart them.

It's kind of like the client "hunting ground" you may experience as a freelancer.

The client, a.k.a. cheetah, puts on a steely gaze as they prowl confidently across the savannah.

Then you, the freelancer, get marked as an easy target.

Craftily, the client decides what technique they're going to use to gain the upper hand and capture you as prey.

They size you up on the spot: have you been eating? How hungry are you?

Then they stealthily make their move.

But you, the nimble and fast-footed copywriter, a.k.a. impala, are on to the cheetah's game… and able to stay one step ahead.

You whip out your favorite tricks to disarm them and catch them by surprise.

You're not what they expected.

They realize this isn't going to be so easy!

You start to gain their respect.

They become awed by your "badassery."

And now, as a result, they want to capture you even more.

That's when the power balance shifts… and you make your move.

Once this little dance is over (it can all happen in just seconds), you're on a more equal footing.

No longer cheetah versus impala…

But client and copywriter working together in a professional, respectful, and win/win relationship.

As it should be!

And this book is going to show you how to do just that.

So let's turn the page and dive in… and I'll see you out on the savannah!

Chapter 1

Figuring Out Your Path to Freelance Success

S ales and marketing have always seemed a bit "sketchy" to some folks. Back when I was a high school senior and told my parents I wanted to go into marketing, their reaction was one of deep disappointment.

I know my parents meant well, and wanted what they thought was best for me: a secure, respectable career.

But I might as well have told them I wanted to dig ditches or empty trash cans for a living (not that this isn't important work... I'm looking out my window now as trash collectors do their weekly pickup and the electric company digs holes in a neighbor's yard across the street).

They told me marketing was "beneath" me, and that it was all about sales and knocking on doors and going on overnight business trips where men would "come onto me" (yes, their exact words!)

What they thought marketing was all about was nothing like what I'd been told earlier that evening when I attended a career fair at my high school outside Dayton, Ohio.

1

About a dozen or so parents staffed various booths, each with a sign on the front listing the profession they worked in: "Doctor"... "Lawyer"... "Engineer"... etc.

Students lined up at the different booths to talk to the parents working in these fields to learn more about these potential careers.

After all, many of us were headed to college and deciding on our majors. Our suburban upper-middle-class parents had blithely sent us off to figure out our own fates... from a carefully-curated set of choices (no ditch-diggers or sanitation workers in the bunch).

At the career fair, I looked around and saw long lines for the well-known, high-paying, parent-approved professions like "doctor" and "lawyer."

Then I looked over to my right and saw a sign that said "Marketing"... and a friendly-looking man standing there. With no line.

In fact, there wasn't anyone waiting to talk with him at all.

I felt sorry for the guy and figured I'd go over and talk with him. I asked him what marketing was and what he did.

Turns out he was a product manager for Mead Corporation, headquartered right up the road in downtown Dayton.

And he began passionately explaining what his job entailed.

How he'd come up with an idea for a new notebook or planner. How he'd do market research to determine who his target customer was and what they needed. How he'd work with the product development team to actually create the new notebook. How he'd coordinate with the advertising department to create the packaging and promotion strategy.

And then, in his own increasingly enthusiastic words, what a great feeling it was to walk into a store and see your notebook on the shelf for sale!

I heard a bell go off in my head: *"Ding Ding Ding Ding Ding!"*

And I knew right then and there that marketing was my calling.

But, as I mentioned at the beginning of this story, my parents shot this idea down in flames. I began to doubt what I had heard and ended up going in a different direction in college.

Despite those doubts, I always knew in the back of my mind that I would get into marketing someday. And eventually, I found out about copywriting... something I "fell into", like the majority of other copywriters I know. (Maybe that's the case for you?)

Yet as much as I feel marketing can be a noble profession just in itself...

...where it's all about, as the late Bob King, president of the publishing division I once worked for, put it: *"Making people better off in ways they desire"*...

...I also know not everyone who puts up a shingle and sells products is in it for the right reasons.

And this is important to remember not just as a consumer, but as a freelance copywriter.

Close the door on the bad to make room for the good

If anything, my parents' initial doubts and concerns turned out to be instructive once I became a freelance copywriter.

Because there are a lot of sham artists and con men (and women) and even men who will hit on you that you WILL encounter.

Your #1 goal is to spot these "clients from hell" before you spend a minute working with them, or even offering up a quote.

Every one of these time-wasting, misery-wreaking clients takes away your time and energy that could have been better spent finding and working with great clients worthy of your skills.

Great clients can be companies who are already recognized leaders in their niche. They can be passionate entrepreneurs with a

3

powerful vision that excites you. They can be solopreneurs who genuinely want to make a difference in other people's lives.

The more you believe in what they're doing, and see their commitment to running their business in an ethical fashion, the more attractive of a client they become.

My feeling is if I'm working for a company or person who really believes in their products… and is committed to helping people use them to improve their lives… it always makes me feel better about working for them.

It's those companies or people who make it clear they're pretty much just in it for the money that make me want to run in the opposite direction.

In my experience, those who have NO problem "screwing over" their customers will have NO problem screwing over you.

Don't beat yourself up if you're not able to discern this characteristic in a client before you start working with them. But DO make sure you do your due diligence before taking on a new client, especially if they are completely unknown to you.

This is where building up your copywriter network also becomes valuable. Being able to reach out to other copywriters who've worked with a particular client can help reveal any hidden "red flags" before you commit to a project.

We'll get into all of this, and much more, in the pages ahead. And in chapter 4, I'll help you spot the 7 types of nightmare clients to avoid (and what to do if you end up working with them).

Yes, we're just getting started.

Maybe you're just getting started with this whole freelance copywriting thing, too.

Or maybe you've been doing it for years… and have the battle scars to prove it.

I've coached copywriters at both stages and everywhere in-between. Even if you are a seasoned copywriter, it makes sense to step back periodically and evaluate your business. Doing so with a trusted mentor can often help you get rid of your blind spots.

Another key thing to remember (and what may be one of the main reasons you got into this whole freelancing thing in the first place): **YOU are the umpire of your own life.**

(Hat tip to top direct response marketer Brian Kurtz, who I'm proud to call a mentor, for this spot-on analogy. I think this is a universal truth for everyone, not just freelancers and others who are self-employed.)

Ultimately, it's YOU who gets to decide what kind of work you'll take on, which clients you'll work with, how much you'll earn, and how much time you want to spend working (or not!)

Obviously, the better you get at what you do, and the more adept you become at handling clients like a "badass," the better options you'll have to choose from—and the more you'll become the umpire of your own life.

So let's talk about some of those options you may be facing right now for your freelance copywriting business…

To niche or not to niche… is that *really* the question?

Deciding to focus on a particular niche depends on where you are now as a freelance copywriter… and where you've been.

You don't have to commit to a niche when you are just starting out as a copywriter. After all, you'll want to get your "reps" in as much as possible with a wide variety of projects, based on what you're able to do for clients and get paid.

Getting paid to write ANY kind of copy will teach you far more than creating multiple "practice" promos in one particular chosen niche (though you should still do these when you're learning about copywriting).

5

It teaches you not just how to handle clients, but gives you the versatility to work on different types of copy (i.e., emails, landing pages, Google or Facebook ads) for a variety of different products.

This forces you to quickly master the research and copywriting know-how needed to attack each new project. And by doing so, gain the confidence you need, as well as those all-important copy samples.

At the same time, you can focus on studying and mastering a particular niche (like financial or supplements), and focus on those types of clients as you gain more experience.

Of course, if you've got deep experience in a particular niche—like I did when I first started freelancing after launching and running a supplement business for a large publisher—then you may want to focus on a particular niche early on.

Either way...

The sooner you can start getting paid, the better!

Most of us don't have the luxury of spending endless time studying how to write copy and creating practice assignments (let alone waste precious hours on "spec" projects that go nowhere—more on that in Chapter 8).

We need to "bring home the bacon," too!

Plus, just like a business needs capital to invest in its growth, you need to invest in your growth as a freelancer.

The sooner you can get to the point that you're able to invest in your training, get yourself a mentor, and build your network by attending live events, the better. These are steps that can really fast-forward your freelance career.

The other thing to remember is, there are a ton of copywriting niches out there. You hear a lot about supplements and financial. But there are successful, 6+ figure careers to be had in everything from SaaS (software as a service) to corporate training to skin care, coaching, survival, fitness, dog food and snacks… you name it.

All of these companies—big, small, and in-between—need copy. We're all reading and watching more ads than ever before, thanks to the Internet and smartphones. There are more businesses selling more things than ever before.

And they all need copy for those sales pages, emails, landing pages, websites, ads, direct mail, and video scripts. There's a whole sea of clients out there waiting to hire you who need your services.

But if you already have deep experience and knowledge in one particular area, your best bet—at least initially—may be to focus on that.

You will be ten times more valuable to a client than someone who doesn't have that unique or relevant background… versus trying to compete in a crowded, competitive niche in which you have little to no experience.

When I left Phillips Publishing after launching and running the Healthy Directions business, finding supplement clients was a breeze. But if I hadn't had that experience, it would have been much more of an uphill battle.

So perhaps your best bet is to let your niche choose YOU… that's what I did!

Eventually, after writing both health and financial copy for years, I decided since I was mostly doing health and supplement copy—with the occasional financial promo popping up and then forcing me to "re-learn" what was going on in the market and where investors' heads were at—I decided to "niche down" to health and supplement copy.

But mind you, this was after nearly 10 years of freelancing! And I still branched out into skin care, fitness, or even the occasional financial promo to keep things interesting.

My advice is to not feel pressured to "niche." Pursue the opportunities that are most relevant to your background and experience... and if something else calls to you, go for that as well.

But get as much paying work as soon as you can, as it will be what truly helps you learn and succeed early on.

Now here's another common question I'm asked by freelance copywriters who are just getting started in their careers. They want to know which type of copy it's best to focus on first...

Should you focus on short or long copy?

Writing long-form sales pages and VSLs is difficult even for experienced copywriters. And some people don't have the bandwidth or want to bother with them at all.

I definitely recommend starting out with shorter copy, like emails (and deciding later if that's what you want to stick with).

Shorter copy is less intimidating to learn, you can often get faster feedback on the results, and you can turn it around faster (and get paid faster... rather than a long-form copy project that can drag out for months, while your rent, mortgage or other bills need to get paid every 30 days!)

Many copywriters decide that writing shorter copy works best for them over the long term. There are plenty of lucrative opportunities to work with a company and run their email marketing for them... and get a "revenue share" deal that can pay you 10% of sales or even more, on top of a monthly retainer. I'll get more into this later.

Or you may specialize in a niche where long-form copy generally isn't used or needed... like SaaS (software as a service) or e-commerce businesses. (Though it never hurts to test new approaches versus doing what everyone else is doing!)

Whatever you end up writing, make sure you focus on this one thing:

Get "dangerously good" at writing copy

As any top-level copywriter will tell you, copywriting is hard. It takes years, even decades, to get really good.

I remember once running into someone who ran a publishing company when I was a freelance copywriter still in my thirties. He told me "Copywriters don't get good until they're at least 45."

Of course, there are always huge exceptions (and I had some big successes under my belt well before that age).

For some people, the lead time is far faster, but it's often directly related to your innate talent for it… plus the hard work you do to learn and master your craft.

Don't just settle for getting good… get "dangerously good." Learn everything you can from as many people as you can. Go back decades and learn from the greats.

Every time you write copy and turn it in to a client, make sure it's as good as it can be. Commit yourself to producing excellent work. Never "half-ass" anything.

The kind of copywriters I've seen succeed the most do all of these things consistently. They don't ever rest on their laurels. Even if they've already proven themselves to be good copywriters, they still do the hard work on their own to constantly read, study, and keep getting better at what they do.

So, to get "dangerously good" at copywriting, it's important to do these 3 things:

1. **Be a good writer**—be able to write clearly and convincingly about anything.
2. **Read and study and understand the classics**—books by Claude Hopkins, Gene Schwartz, Robert Cialdini, John Caples, and others. Know the strategies that build the foundation of a successful ad or promotion.

3. **Forget about "formulas."** While you should make use of proven tools and strategies, there is no "paint by numbers" recipe you can simply use without coming up with mediocre results at best.

The best way to produce and understand what great copy is—even as AI tools become more and more sophisticated—is to develop a deep mastery of the fundamentals of copywriting.

For example, knowing what makes for a great headline. How to use curiosity to compel someone to open your email or read your sales page. The techniques of building a case for buying your product and differentiating it from its competition.

And then knowing when to bend the rules when it benefits your unique ad or promo.

As the great artist Pablo Picasso once said, *"Learn the rules like a pro, so you can break them like an artist."*

That's why, rather than simply applying a formula or using AI-generated output, it's best to understand exactly why it works and how other successful "artists" apply it to their winning promotions.

Hopefully, I've told you some things you didn't already know. Unlike the sugar-coating and sales pitches you may hear from others, copywriting isn't an easy way to make money. It takes talent, commitment, hard work, and resilience to succeed.

As you read in the Introduction, I don't shy away from being blunt and telling it "like it is."

Especially if you're holding up dinner.

Chapter 2

Client-Finding Techniques to Keep You Plenty Busy (and Not Needy)

There are more opportunities for freelance copywriters than ever before. But there's also more competition.

You'll definitely give yourself a huge edge when you commit to becoming "dangerously good" at copywriting… always producing excellent work… being great to work with… and developing a track record of results.

Over time (or you could be at this point now), you'll have clients coming to you. There are ways to have this happen consistently, which I'll get to in a moment.

Many years ago when I beat the late Jim Rutz, a legendary direct response copywriter, and beat another big-name copywriter shortly thereafter to become the first female copywriter to get a Boardroom control (it was one of the most elite direct response publishers to write for at the time, known for only working with the top A-listers), it helped put me "on the map"… and kept plenty of client work coming my way.

(Note: a "control" refers to a promo, typically long-form—though it can refer to emails and other ads as well—that is the primary ad or promo that a company runs for a particular product. Just like a scientist who conducts experiments using a control versus different test panels, direct marketers will often test new ads or promos against their current control, and smart ones are always looking to beat it!)

Back when I was starting out as a freelance copywriter, there was no social media (this makes me feel like a dinosaur). There weren't easy ways to build an email list or post regularly on a blog or otherwise get yourself "known." There was no Upwork or Fiverr.

Now there are plenty of ways to leverage social media, like Facebook copywriting groups and LinkedIn, in order to find clients. You can comment on posts and share insights that demonstrate your knowledge and value. You can network and even get on an actual call with a potential client or fellow copywriter who may be a good contact.

But there are some timeless tactics that work as well as—or likely, much better—than these social media techniques. And they can work whether you're just starting out or you've got a full client roster —but want to keep new, better ones in the pipeline.

How to leverage the power of referrals to fill up your schedule

The best way to get new clients when you're starting out is to let everyone know you're a copywriter. Chances are you've had some prior work experience, maybe within a company that also has to market and advertise their products.

Guess what? They could be your first client! My former employer became one of my biggest clients the year after I walked out the door on good terms (always avoid burning bridges).

There's also the power of referrals to tap into. Being referred by someone else drastically increases your odds of getting hired by a client. Even better, it helps you charge higher fees, because they feel more confident about your abilities.

Make an exhaustive list of all the people you know who could possibly refer you to a potential client. Your list could include:

- Friends you attended college with.
- Former coworkers and bosses.
- Friends or neighbors who work for various companies.
- Any past clients you've done work for, or...
- People you've gotten to "know" on social media (perhaps in copywriting groups where you've contributed value or when people mention extra work to offload).

As you can see, chances are you know more people than you think who can refer you. And it's my favorite way to bring on new clients.

That's because *anytime* someone refers you... especially if they say things like "s/he's a great copywriter" or "great to work with"... your "stock" goes up exponentially with a potential client.

And, like I mentioned before, if it's someone they trust who's referring you, you may find it very easy to close them AND get a higher fee.

Obviously, that's contingent on you handling things professionally, demonstrating attention to detail and a strong command of the English language, and having relevant samples to show the potential client.

But don't automatically take on someone to be a client just because someone has referred them. You still want to do the usual "vetting" to make sure they're someone you want to work with.

(It's always helpful to ask the person who referred you how they know the client and if they've worked with them in the past. If they've done so and the experience was good, then they've helped do some of the vetting for you in advance.)

Side note: Make sure you show your appreciation to people who refer you to a client, especially a good one that you land a project with. A hand-written thank you note, and/or a gift (like fruit, cheese, snacks, flowers, frozen steaks… that kind of thing) goes a long way toward making people want to keep referring you to others.

Build a thriving freelance business… by going in-house?

It might sound like anathema when you're looking to build a thriving freelance business.

But one of the best ways to break into freelance copywriting is to consider working as an employee for an established direct response company first for a year or two (I'll get more into this in chapter 11).

Many companies are looking for entry-level copywriters and other talent, all the way up to more senior positions. And these days, they're often fine with 100% remote workers.

Being an in-house employee lets you build an incredibly valuable network of referrals you can tap into later. Plus, it also gives you the opportunity to get feedback from more experienced people on your copy… get access to the results data that many freelance clients aren't willing to share… and get paid to learn!

When I first left Phillips Publishing to become a freelance copywriter, not only were there people who still worked there who referred me to clients… some had moved on to other jobs and ended up referring me to their new employers or hiring me themselves!

So going in-house can be a great way to boost your network over the long-term and get valuable experience. You'll get bonus benefits if the company you go to work for is seen as a leader in your niche… because that can really open doors once you go freelance! Again, I'll get into this more later as well as some of the traps you'll want to avoid.

Speaking of which, here's one of the most enjoyable and lucrative client-hunting grounds where you'll also step up your copywriting and marketing know-how…

How to get a 500% ROI by attending events (and have fun doing so!)

Whenever you can, it's important to crawl out of that cave and meet people via events, online mastermind groups, and copywriter communities. The #1 best way I've met clients has been by attending in-person events and masterminds.

I get that most of these programs do require investments that may not be viable for you.

But I would suggest that when you are able to do so, investing in attending a conference, for example, may well provide an **ROI** of at least 2 to 5 times the cost of attending (and I'm factoring in airfare, hotel, and meals, too).

That's true as long as you use your time there in the most valuable way possible.

For starters, always sit next to people you don't know and don't be shy about striking up conversations.

Conferences are one of the most welcoming places in the world to do so. And you'd be amazed how many mutually-profitable "on the fly" conversations happen this way.

At one large marketing event, I joined a table of strangers during lunch and ended up sitting next to Joe Sugarman, an industry legend and founder of Blu Blockers, and who's sadly no longer with us. This led to a client referral from Joe himself!

I've met other folks who turned into being great clients just by sitting next to them and chatting before a speaker takes the stage... including a woman who's a major player in the supplement and skin care industry who I've been working with recently.

Same is true for meals, whether they're included at the event or you need to grab lunch or dinner on your own. Don't be shy about asking someone to join you or asking if you can join them and their group.

You can also initiate spontaneous "hey, let's grab lunch or dinner" groups that you pull together during session breaks.

Yes, even if you are naturally an introvert, you can do this... (I am, and these are all things I've done multiple times. It gets easier the more often you do it!)

The "cost-cutting" tactic that could cost you valuable client connections

One more tip: it's always worth paying a little extra to stay at the "official" conference hotel.

First off, there are the spontaneous conversations that can lead to potential clients that happen just riding up and down in the elevators or walking through the lobby.

And at night, you'll typically find fellow conference attendees hanging out in the hotel bar. This can be by far the most effective and lucrative client-finding you do!

Note: Don't get drunk! You want to be in control of how you present yourself. If you're sipping glasses of tonic water and lime, no one will know the difference.

That's why the #1 rule when you attend an event is to spend as little time as possible holed up in your hotel room.

Do NOT plan on working while you're there... you want to show up at as many sessions as possible (and not be completely focused on your laptop), and make the most of the other networking opportunities I've mentioned here.

Hopefully, these tips and tactics will help you book up your schedule with new, high-quality clients... and get more out of the client-finding efforts you're doing now. But remember...

There's no need to go it alone!

Make sure you work on your referral network as much as possible. You likely know more people than you think who either know or could become potential clients.

Even if you feel you have a robust referral network, you should still constantly grow and nurture it. One way to do so is to join select copywriter communities.

I say "select" because there are some social media groups where scammy would-be clients are lurking, or where everyone seems to be in the same desperate place.

One of my favorite Facebook groups with a positive, helpful vibe is The Copywriter Club. The founders, Rob Marsh and Kira Hug, keep the community focused on supporting each other, and provide many valuable resources and growth opportunities.

And a great paid community you may want to consider joining is Copy Chief, founded by top copywriter Kevin Rogers—who also happens to be a fantastic mentor.

Copy Chief offers a wide range of training opportunities, chances to get your copy critiqued, and boasts one of the industry's most robust job boards. It's become a go-to spot for top direct response companies looking for freelance and in-house copywriters.

Of course, there's no substitute for being in face-to-face situations with other people... and you really could meet one of your "dream" clients at a conference or other event.

But there are other ways to get your foot in the door without ponying up a big conference fee and paying to travel. I'll cover them in the next chapter, so keep reading!

Chapter 3

Finding and Landing that "Dream" Client (They DO Exist!)

M aybe you've had your eye on a potential client, and you've tried getting your foot in the door without success.

Or perhaps you've done work with a past client you enjoyed working with and you'd like to do more.

For any of these situations, I'm about to reveal some tactics you can use to line up new client projects starting right now… and maybe even land that "dream" client.

But I'm going to first illustrate them with a seemingly unrelated story…

Back when I was a young single professional (1980s term: "yuppie") living in Baltimore, I was in a group house one summer with a bunch of friends in Rehoboth Beach, Delaware—about a 3-hour drive away.

Rehoboth, along with Dewey Beach, the next town over, was where hordes of 20 and 30-somethings from the Baltimore and Washington, DC area went to hang out on the weekends.

One Labor Day weekend, I had a girlfriend from Chicago visiting and we headed down to the beach house. The first night, a group of us headed to the popular bayfront bar, the Rusty Rudder.

Shortly thereafter, one friend noticed a guy checking me out from afar. I shrugged it off as the whole summer I'd gotten sick of guys hitting on me, and besides, my friend was in from out of town and I wanted to catch up with her.

A bit later, my friend and I broke off from the group and were talking near the dance floor, where a reggae band was playing. The same aforementioned guy decides to make his approach.

He comes up and says, *"Dance with me."*

I felt like it was a little "presumptive" and I wasn't in the mood to dance, so I replied, "Not now, maybe later."

He hesitated a moment, then sadly walked away.

A few minutes after that, my friend and I each decided to do a shot of tequila. The aforementioned guy witnessed us doing so.

A few minutes after, he walks up and says, *"I've been watching you all night and think you're gorgeous. Will you dance with me?"*

My answer this second time around was, "Sure!" (As I handed my friend my purse to hold while I danced.)

And that, my friends, was how I met my husband.

Who ended up taking me out to dinner a few nights later for our first date, and who I saw every weekend throughout our courtship until we got married nearly 30 years ago.

So let's take a quick look at the marketing and copywriting lessons here, shall we?

Life lessons you can also apply to finding clients

This example of how I met my husband showcases several valuable lessons that can help you generate more sales with your copy and marketing efforts—and find clients:

Lesson #1: Never give up on a prospect after making the initial offer. You often need to get your offer in front of a prospect multiple times before they buy. Persistence pays! Sometimes it's just the mere repetition of the same offer, coming from multiple channels, that finally convinces a prospect to act.

Lesson #2: Just because your prospect says "no" now doesn't mean they will later. You never know exactly at what point your prospect will be most receptive to your offer. Conditions can change. They may not want your cholesterol supplement offer right now, but six months later, after their next annual physical, they might be all over it.

Lesson #3: Test your copy—always! Just because one headline (or opening sentence) doesn't work doesn't mean something else won't either. Test short copy ("Dance with me") versus long copy ("I've been watching you all night and I think you're gorgeous...") and see what happens. (Hint: longer copy almost always wins!)

Lesson #4: Make sure your messaging speaks to your prospect's desires and emotions. The line that flopped ("Dance with me") has nothing in it for the prospect, whereas the one that worked used the age-old technique of flattering the prospect (vanity is a powerful emotion).

Definitely some good lessons here... plus a fun trip down memory lane for me. So how can these same lessons apply to booking up your schedule with high-quality clients?

Because playing "hard to get" often has the highly profitable effect of making clients want you even more since you're "unavailable." It even makes them quicker and more willing to send over those fat advance checks to reserve a slot in your ever-more-crowded schedule.

(And an invitation to dance goes over much more smoothly once a tequila shot has been consumed! Yes, timing *is* everything.)

Next up, I'm going to share a strategy you can use to land that dream client you've been dying to work with. It's a highly-profitable secret one of my friends (who is also a top A-list copywriter) shared with folks on a coaching call I hosted a few years back.

His advice for landing that "big fish" client that you want to reel in is to remember this…

We're in the business of "ideas"… and so are our clients

Companies that sell supplements, health newsletters, financial advisories, and other products via direct marketing are always looking for that next big idea that can SELL.

It's not just a matter of breaking through the noise and clutter of promotions that are constantly hitting your prospect from all directions and grabbing their attention.

It needs to be a big enough idea that it's got "legs." It needs to be such a powerful and engaging idea and promise, it gets our increasingly distracted prospect to read it, not just click on it.

There are plenty of classic examples, like David Ogilvy's famous print ad for Rolls Royce with the headline: "At 60 miles an hour the loudest noise in the new Rolls-Royce comes from the electric clock."

Apparently, Ogilvy produced 26 different headlines for the ad, and then got half a dozen writers from the agency to go over them and pick out the best one.

They chose the headline I shared with you—which perfectly illustrates the company's attention to detail and luxury. Rolls Royce's sales jumped 50% within one year, making it one of the most successful ad campaigns ever.

Some of the world's best copywriters on the planet have tried and failed to come up with successful ideas like these. That's because due to highly-saturated markets and the increasingly intense competition for attention, it's gotten harder and more challenging than ever to come up with ideas that stand out.

But it happens all the time that someone, perhaps someone who's never been heard of outside of a teensy-tiny Facebook copywriting group, hits on something they convinced a company to try... and comes up with a huge winner.

So here's what you do if you want to try to get your "big break"... or if you're an established copywriter looking to get your foot in the door with a dream client.

It's the same strategy this A-lister told me he used to land a new project with a longtime client. In fact, he ended up getting a hot new control with it, by beating a previously "unbeatable" control written years earlier by another top A-list copywriter:

Come up with what you think could be that next control-slaying "big idea" for that client.

Read everything you can that their company puts out. Research what's going on in their space—newsworthy things, what the competition is doing, new developments, etc.

And then...

Start brainstorming!

If something grabs you and makes you stop and say, "wait, that's interesting..." then it very well may have the same effect on a prospect (and your prospective client).

In our increasingly bizarre world where we're seeing things that we never thought we'd see in our lifetimes, when you can hit on something that stops you in your tracks, you know you're onto something!

Now take that idea, flesh it out some more, look for some back-up or proof. Then write out some possible headlines and short leads that could work with it—or find some other way to "demonstrate" the idea, i.e., a copy platform synopsis.

Then send that to your prospective or past client. (Side note: if it's a client you've never worked with before, see if someone in your network can provide their email address, or sometimes Google knows what it is. Or you can try reaching out via social media messaging, i.e., LinkedIn.)

Let the person know you're following their company's promotions (you'll want to be getting their free e-letters and even buy their product or subscribe to their newsletter). And that you're interested in and passionate about the subject matter.

Share just enough of your fleshed-out idea to get them intrigued (don't give away the store to protect your interests). Oh, and only do this with a potential client or company you trust won't rip you off and go do your idea themselves. It needs to be a company with integrity.

And then see what happens. Follow up after a week or so, since a lot of emails do get buried or end up in spam folders.

If they don't bite after a few follow-ups, move on. According to my fellow A-lister friend, who works with a lot of major publishers, this is a great technique for breaking in with a new client, or reactivating a past one.

Even if it doesn't result in a project, it's a great exercise for you to go through if you're somewhat new to copywriting. That's because this is the hardest (and most crucial) step in writing a new promotion: coming up with good ideas and angles.

There are a lot of people in the world who can string together a bunch of words and call themselves a "copywriter". But the real superstars are the ones that find the best ideas and turn them and the right words into breakthrough multi-million-dollar promotions.

Figuring out who your "dream" clients are

Maybe you're not sure which potential clients you should be aiming for in the first place. Or maybe you've got plenty of client work, but not with clients that come anywhere near "dream" status.

The first step to building a more profitable copywriting business is figuring out WHO your dream clients are. Eventually, you'll reach a point where you no longer just take any gig that comes your way. You'll want to start only working with your favorite kind of clients. But before this big mindset shift can ever happen, you have to start getting super-clear on WHO it is you'd like to work with.

A useful exercise for setting your sights on higher-quality clients is to make a "Dream 100" list. This is an exercise I heard about from top email copywriter Chris Orzechowski.

Chris actually adapted it from the exercise David Ogilvy did when he first started his advertising agency. Apparently, Ogilvy made a list of 5 big accounts that would be his "dream clients." And by the end of his career, he managed to sign all 5.

Who knows? Maybe this exercise can do the same for you.

Regardless, it's going to help you get really clear on the type of clients you'd like to work for, what characteristics they all share, and how you can market yourself so that the companies you list here would be interested in hiring someone like you.

Step #1: Make your "Dream 100" List

Make a list of your 100 DREAM clients. Don't just think about what companies you can get a gig with now. Think about which companies you'd love to be able to work with someday. No dream is too far-fetched. Give yourself permission to go a little crazy here and dream big!

Step #2: What do they have in common?

Take a look at your list of dream clients. Are there any commonalities between them?

If they don't ALL share the exact same characteristics, are there patterns you see emerging?

What kind of industries are these clients in? What kind of products do they sell? How big are these businesses? Is there a problem they all seem to have, based on what you know about the market or industry? Ask yourself these questions and more.

Step #3: Identify your solutions

Now that you've got your list, and you've looked at the problems and characteristics these companies have in common, it's time to identify your solutions.

Ask yourself what kind of work could you see yourself doing for these companies. It's okay if you're not an expert at this kind of work right now. But think about what kind of problems you'd like to solve for them, what kind of results you'd like to deliver, and what you'd have to do in order to make that happen. Write it all out on a piece of paper.

Hopefully, after doing this exercise (and it's fine if you can't identify 100... 10 or 20 would be a great start), you'll have more clarity about the clients you want to be focusing on, and how to best position yourself to work with them.

Now, in the next chapter, I'm going to tell you about the types of clients you DON'T want to be working with. Many of them are based on my own personal "school of hard knocks" training. Hopefully, I can spare you from some of the same agony.

Chapter 4

7 Types of Clients You Meet on the Road to Copywriting "Hell"

No matter where you find clients, or even if they're referred to you by others, you still need to screen them and pay attention to anything that gives you pause.

That's why now I want to talk about some of the biggest client "warning signs" to watch out for. I call them the *7 types of clients you meet on the road to copywriting "Hell."*

Think of them as big red flashing lights that scream "DANGER!"... and ignore them at your own peril. Let's start with...

Client Nightmare #1: Hasn't worked with a copywriter before

If you're working with a "newbie" client—and they're a virgin when it comes to working with copywriters —prepare yourself for lots of hand-holding, anxiety attacks, and control issues. "High-maintenance" doesn't even begin to cover it all.

One thing to keep in mind is if your client hasn't ever worked with a copywriter, chances are they're a fairly new start-up and don't have much of a budget. So they probably aren't going to be able to afford a more experienced copywriter to lead the way.

Now, this can be a great opportunity for a "greener" copywriter who wants to gain experience and get a big win or two under their belt. But tread carefully.

Because chances are this client doesn't fully understand the value of copy, or thinks they can write it themselves (see Client Nightmare #2).

And whatever they're paying you may seem like a LOT to them. So there's a good chance they'll dither over your copy far too long with nit-picky changes so they can feel "in control." Not to mention expect that you guarantee or assure them it's going to work!

If, despite all these red flags, you decide to move forward with this type of client, pay close attention to the client management tactics in this book from the get-go, so you can set yourself up as a trusted advisor they can't push around.

Build in extra time and charge a bit more if you can, since this project may not move as quickly along as most—and will likely require more of your time. But if it's the right client and you do a good job, they could end up being a dream client over the long-term.

Client Nightmare #2: Thinks they're a good copywriter

This client may actually BE a good copywriter, but they've let it go to their head too much. I once had a client I'd started working with who from the start talked about wanting to hire me to work in-house (sorry, that wasn't going to happen, buddy!)

Then, in a follow-up conversation, he suggested he write his own version of a promo we were discussing having me write, and then do a head-to-head copy test.

This felt more like his ego talking than anything else. After all, he was the president of the company. Why spend your time writing copy when you can hire ME to do it? Yikes.

Another variation on this type of client is the solopreneur who's deciding whether to write their own copy, or hire a copywriter to do it. Obviously, they feel confident enough about their own copywriting skills to write their own copy, but they don't want to spend time doing it themselves.

Yet when it comes to actually hiring you and paying you to do it, they back out. All too often, they'll milk ideas out of you on calls and string you along—only to ghost you.

Now, this "good copywriter syndrome" isn't always a negative. One of my best clients is someone who was a highly successful copywriter before he went on to launch a publishing and supplement biz.

And any time we've worked together, while he may have strong opinions on certain things that ultimately don't matter a whole lot (more like personal preference stuff), he also contributes great ideas and feedback, making for a highly profitable collaboration.

The bottom line is, make sure you proceed slowly and carefully... and don't make too big of a commitment with this type of client until you get to know them better.

Client Nightmare #3: The "boot-strapping" client

I remember talking a few times by phone with a potential client who was referred by someone well-known in the direct marketing world. This client had worked with some successful companies and was now branching out on his own.

Turns out we were both going to be at a major marketing conference, so we arranged an in-person meet up. We situated ourselves in two comfy chairs in the hotel lobby.

This is someone who seemed to know every direct marketing "bro" that walked by as we chatted. Then we finally got to the topic we'd all but avoided while he rhapsodized on and on about this big amazing business he was launching: how much $$ did I want?

It was then that he used that fateful word: "boot-strapping"... yammering on about how they were "boot-strapping" the business and couldn't afford to pay much. So why are you talking to me, bro?

Look, perhaps this could have been a chance to get equity in something I would help build. But that doesn't pay the mortgage or the kids' private school or college bills.

And it's often simply used as a lure that rarely delivers. I heard from another copywriter who ended up working with this client later. He described his experience as nothing less than a "total sh*t show" and was getting out ASAP. Another client "landmine" avoided!

You deserve to be paid and have your copy seen as a crucial lever or investment when building a business. Not something where you have little to no control, yet your fate (and your future compensation) hangs on the whims and dealings of someone else... not to mention an unproven offer or product.

Get your money or tell them to go hire someone else. If you want to build in some kind of "at risk" bonus or revenue share or royalty, that's fine... but make sure you've got a big enough upfront fee built in to compensate you for your time in addition to incentives.

Client Nightmare #4: The flip-flopping client

The flip-flopping client often shows their hand before you even start working with them.

They may lean on you for suggestions and attempt to "pick your brain" incessantly before committing to a project. This, in itself, is a warning sign of what likely comes later.

That's because as soon as you diligently start working on their project (which, in many cases, you've helped them define), they tell you they want to take a different approach.

Their indecisiveness and flip-flopping often results from a lack of confidence. Many solopreneurs (not all) may fall into this category.

Their self-doubt can be amplified by their insecure need to constantly follow what everyone else is doing in their mastermind and keep up with the Joneses, even if it's not the best strategy for their business.

The flip-flopping client can also be a low-level or middle-management type at a large company. They may be dealing with a boss that's constantly changing their mind, or upper-level management that wants a "change in direction" or has somehow screwed their relationship with a product spokesperson or guru.

Either way, if you're stuck in the middle of a project with one of these flip-flopping clients, expect to be put through multiple rounds of revisions, corporate indecision, and—in those big company scenarios—conflicting feedback from multiple people that will have you pulling your hair out.

You can rein some of this madness in pre-emptively by putting limitations on the number of rounds (before charging extra) in your contract.

But even then, a project that goes on for weeks and months after it's supposed to have wrapped up can wreak havoc with your schedule, leaving you overlapping that work with new client projects you've already scheduled... and a delayed final invoice you'd love to be able to send so you can get paid.

This leaves you with the prospect of either working overtime for weeks on end to juggle both projects... or informing that other client you need to push back to a later start date, potentially damaging that relationship.

This is why, if you can sniff out a flip-flopper BEFORE you commit to working with them, you'll save yourself from this time-sucking frustration that causes far more trouble than it's worth in the long run.

Client Nightmare #5: The creepy-crawly "scope creep" client

A close relative to the flip-flopping client is the dreaded "scope creep" client. While they are a similar species, the "scope creep" client can often be easier to spot up front.

That's why if you find yourself in the nightmare clutches of this client vermin, you'll likely be able to pinpoint the early warning signs you missed as you kick yourself repeatedly.

It often starts early in the project proposal phase. As you're close to clarifying the project with the client in a call or via email, they throw in what seems like a harmless request. It could be writing a few additional paragraphs of ad copy, or an extra version of an email.

Because you want to close the deal and it won't take much extra time to do what they've asked, you may find yourself agreeing. But with this type of client, it's like opening the floodgates to a succession of requested "freebies."

Anything that takes you extra time to produce for a client is something you should be charging for... since your time is money. I will say things get a bit "fuzzy" when you're doing a project with royalty potential or other financial incentives.

But it's still important to rein things in and have a clearly defined project scope written into your contract.

For example, even for a royalty-type deal, I'll clarify exactly what "ancillary" copy I'll produce as part of the initial project in addition to the long-form sales page or other promo.

"Ancillary" copy is a broad category that increasingly more clients are heaping additional copy needs under: lifts (emails that drive traffic), Google or Facebook ads, sponsorship ads, website copy, the list goes on and on.

Then there's the funnel copy that may be impossible to map out completely in advance without creating the entire strategy for the client, and without them paying you for your time to do so, or committing to hiring you to do it.

This reminds me a of a tough lesson I learned the hard way early on. A major publisher was launching their own supplement subsidiary, and asked me for a quote on writing a retention marketing series to get first-time buyers to reorder.

I spent hours putting together a detailed proposal, outlining the strategy and tactics, the different promotions and timing, etc. All of it was based on the multi-million-dollar retention strategies I'd come up with and implemented when I was running the Healthy Directions supplement business.

You know what this prospective client said after I proudly handed in my proposal, confident they'd be so impressed with my detailed strategy that they'd hire me on the spot?

"Thank you for your proposal. We've decided to do it ourselves."

Damn! I felt like an idiot. A completely used and taken-advantage-of idiot at that.

This is why I say again and again: DON'T give away the details of how you'll do something in your proposal... or in that client sales call.

And your best defense against the "scope creep" client is to clearly define the scope as much as possible. Make sure you include a large enough flat fee and incentive potential to cover the inevitable additions that may be thrown in if it's a large project like a launch.

Don't automatically say "yes" to everything. From the start, it's essential you present yourself as a professional whose time and work is valuable... not something you give away for free.

This one tactic alone can help you command the client respect you deserve. But no matter how smart you play it, you may be blindsided like I was when you encounter the next type of client...

Client Nightmare #6: The "horn dog" client who makes sexual advances or remarks

Clients are usually on their best behavior when you first start working together.

But then you suddenly find yourself flying from out of town to meet with them, riding in a car together to go to lunch, and next thing they're saying out of the blue, "Why don't we stop and get a hotel room?"

No, seriously… it happened once to me many years ago. (OKAY, mom and dad… you were right!)

But I was prepared. A few months before this, I'd had a phone conversation with another client where he said something along the lines of maybe he was my "type."

And I'd successfully shut it down immediately with this two-sentence phrase I'd learned at a sexual harassment seminar at the company where I worked before going freelance:

"When you say (do) things like that, it makes me uncomfortable. I want you to stop."

Commit that phrase to memory and pull it out when you need to… like when you're shocked and stunned like I was in that client's car, so that it's the first thing that comes out of your mouth. It's called putting the offending person "on notice."

And it works. Look, both of these incidents happened at least a decade before the "me too" movement. Unfortunately, stuff like that was commonplace (and sadly still is).

But once I confidently and, more importantly, CLEARLY put the kibosh on it, it never happened again with those clients.

I not only went on to work with both of them for many years afterwards, they became some of my best clients from whom I earned a pretty penny in fees and royalties.

What's more, I also earned their respect. They just needed to be put on notice I wasn't putting up with any of their "horn dog" shenanigans.

You can do the same. The sooner the better, but it's also never too late to deal with it, even if you've been so stunned and confused by it, you've tolerated it—until now.

Use that magic two-sentence phrase, and see what happens! It sucks that this is the world we live in, but this should help you deal with it.

Client Nightmare #7: The deadbeat client who pays late or not at all

It's quite possible the deadbeat client is the worst "client from hell" of all.

Here you've produced the copy you promised in good faith. Perhaps because it's a rush job, you jumped in and started working on it without waiting for your advance.

Or you spent days, weeks, or even months finalizing and perfecting the copy after going through multiple rounds of reviews... until it got client approval.

You submit your final invoice and you wait... and you wait... and you wait.

You check your bank account or mailbox with increasing frequency. Meanwhile, those credit card bills and mortgage payments and other expenses keep piling up or becoming due.

I had this happen once after writing a sales page for a client. It was someone I hadn't worked with before, but he was with a fairly well-known company.

The project went smoothly. I'd gotten my 50% advance well before starting on the copy. We went through a few rounds of changes, and then the client approved the copy.

I emailed him my final invoice for the multi-thousand-dollar balance that was due. And then I waited.

No check showed up in my mailbox after a few weeks. So I sent him a follow-up email. And another. And another. No response.

I then sent another email showing concern, and asking if he was okay. Since things had gone smoothly and we had a good rapport, I didn't think he would blow me off like this.

It got to the point that I went online to check the obituaries in his city. *Seriously*. But no, it didn't appear that he had suddenly suffered some sort of tragic accident.

It was time to get serious about collecting the large sum of money this guy's company owed me. So I contacted my lawyer and had him write a demand letter. He then Fedex'ed it to this guy's office address.

A few short days later, I got the check in the mail for the balance owed me. No explanation, but at this point, this client was nothing more than "dust in the wind" to me.

Every seasoned copywriter I know has multiple "deadbeat client" horror stories like this one. It's why I'm glad I took the advice of more experienced copywriters when I first hung up my shingle as a freelance copywriter: ALWAYS get paid at least a 50% advance before you do a lick of work.

Yes, that's true even if it's a rush job… or even if it's a client you've done work with in the past. You may even want to ask for a 100% payment up front.

That's something I do if working with a client abroad (based on one bad experience where someone in another country stiffed me out of a hefty 5-figure amount, and it was too difficult if not impossible to go after it).

Or if I'm doing consulting or copy review work, I get 100% upfront. That's because at least with copy I've written, I can tell them they don't have the rights to use it until I'm paid. But I don't have that same leverage with consulting or copy critiques I've already provided.

Surprisingly, smaller companies are often better about paying you fast than bigger ones. It always boggles my mind when large company clients think they can pay you on "net 30-day" terms. That means that your invoice isn't due until 30 days after it's received.

You are not a big company that can absorb expenses until revenue comes in. You've got to keep a roof over yours (and likely others') heads, and food on the table.

So put on your invoice that it's due upon receipt… or if it's an advance, it's due before work begins or within 7 days of receipt to hold your time.

(Yes, even if the project doesn't start until six months later, your advance is due **NOW** if you're going to reserve a slot in your schedule and turn down other work for that slot in the meantime. You don't want to wait six months, have them suddenly back out, and leave you scrambling to find client work to fill their spot.)

And if they give you that spiel about not being able to "get it through accounting" that fast? Stick to your guns and let them know you can't start until the advance is received.

You'll be amazed how quickly they can suddenly produce that check or process that payment. I've had clients give me that same song and dance, and then magically get the payment into my bank account just hours later.

And if the project is over but they still owe you the balance due?

If you haven't gotten it within a few weeks, send another email with the invoice attached reminding them it's due (they may have forgotten to forward it on for payment). Then give it a little more time, assuming you've gotten assurance from the client that it's being processed.

If, after a few more follow-ups, you don't get the courtesy of a response, don't hesitate to have an attorney send a demand letter… via FedEx or other overnight mail preferably!

These kinds of slow or late-paying clients will put your freelance business practices under the maximum "stress test."

That's why even if you're just starting out, it's crucial you set up firm rules and policies for how and when clients pay you… to avoid crying in your beer later.

You'll be glad you did! It sure beats checking the obituaries to figure out why you haven't gotten paid.

Get good at spotting these nightmare clients *before* you agree to work with them... and save yourself grief later!

Now that you know the 7 types of clients you meet on the road to copywriting "hell," make sure you watch for warning signs and do as much upfront screening as you can.

Chances are, no matter how careful you are, you'll still find yourself dealing with one of these nightmare clients.

They can sneak up and surprise you (like the "horn dog client")… seem like a dream to work with, until that final invoice is due (like the "deadbeat client")…

…make what feels like a reasonable request something you end up regretting later (like the "scope creep" client)… or constantly need reassurance and annoyingly nit-picky revisions (like the "newbie" client who hasn't worked with copywriters before).

But depending on how you handle these sticky situations, they can end up becoming some of your best clients.

Like the "horn dog client" who knows they can't cross certain boundaries, and develops greater respect for you.

Like the "scope creep client" who genuinely values your willingness to go the extra mile, and agrees to pay you more the next time.

Or like the "newbie" client who appreciates the hand-holding you did for them... and starts to see you as a valued partner as their business grows and blossoms.

(That "deadbeat client" though? There's generally no hope for them... unless they really never got your invoice... or they died.)

Often your best bet, though, is to steer clear of these nightmare clients in the first place. I'll give you some tips and tactics you can use to do so in the next chapter.

Chapter 5

Weeding Out Client Nightmares...
Before They Happen

I remember way back when I was interviewing potential nannies after my first child was born more than 25 years ago. I needed a reliable full-time nanny so I could go back to work at the publishing company where I was a marketer.

And let's just say, like many a first-time parent, my standards were exceedingly high.

To save myself time, I'd do most of my screening of candidates over the phone. If something didn't hit me right, I'd move on to the next candidate.

Then, if they sounded pretty good, before I took the time to interview them in person, I'd call at least two or three references.

Any hints of doubt or misgivings were usually answered by the time I took all those steps, and I'd save myself the time and trouble of going any further.

Ultimately, we found a great nanny we had for years... but I had quite a few I had to "weed out" along the way. I followed my gut, and it was right.

You should also listen to your gut when it comes to taking on a potential client.

And now that you know about the 7 types of clients you meet on the road to copywriting hell, hopefully those warning bells will ring so loudly in your head, you can't ignore them.

But sometimes we do anyway.

Do your "due diligence" before working with a new client

Let me share with you what happened to a copywriter friend when she ignored the warning bells that were trying to send her a message.

Here's her nightmare client story...

"The CEO disappeared in the middle of a launch to go to Burning Man, and then the winning product had a 50% refund rate. When I finally tracked down the CEO and asked about his product development team, he blinked at me and said, 'Product development?' Oh, and he wasn't paying his vendors.

"This was one of my first jobs. It taught me a lot about due diligence before accepting someone as a client. It's been years and I still get emails from irate customers looking for this guy."

Now, I've never been to Burning Man. But I can imagine the vast majority of people who go end up experimenting with various substances that frazzle the brain and scramble the memory. And they probably need some time to recover once they get back.

The lesson here—as my copywriter friend summed up so well—is to do your due diligence before working with a new client.

If this potential new client says someone referred you to them, ask who it was. Talk to that person and find out what they know about the potential client and their company. (It's also good to know this because you'll want to thank this person for the referral.)

If the potential client wasn't referred to you by someone else, see if you can find out if you know any people in common. Have they worked with other freelance copywriters before?

If they haven't, that can sometimes be a "red flag"... though not necessarily a deal breaker. Like I said in the last chapter, be prepared to "train" your client a bit and do more handholding than usual.

If it's a pretty substantial project or launch, you may want to take an extra step and ask the client for a reference—another copywriter they've worked with before, for example—and then talk to that copywriter.

I've actually done this on a few occasions before deciding to work (or not) with a prospective new client, and found they were happy to oblige.

If it's a smaller-scale project, and you're not able to properly "vet" the prospective client as well as you'd like, ask for 100% of your fee upfront.

There are many copywriters who do this routinely (like I've said before, I've done it when working with international clients, since chasing them down later for nonpayment isn't worth the hassle).

One other thing... if you find out your client is heading to Burning Man in the middle of your project, make sure you get paid first!

When to fight back and when to walk away

The lesson here is, if you're getting the "willies" about a potential client, it's good to listen to your inner voice.

Even if you feel you really need that project financially, you could end up on the short end of the stick and never see the money that was promised. But perhaps there weren't any obvious warning signs or "red flags"... and you still find yourself on the short end of the stick.

It's often best to just walk away and leave it in your rear-view mirror... versus letting it suck dry your time, energy, and emotional bank account (I'll talk more about this later).

The most important thing is to chalk it up to being a valuable learning experience—and make sure you don't make the same mistake of ignoring your inner voice the next time!

Here's another valuable lesson I learned early on in my business as well as freelance career. It's one of my own nightmare client stories (and in retrospect, pretty funny)...

Treat others like crap, and you'll get CRAP

Before I went freelance, I was fortunate enough to work for companies and bosses that allowed employees free range to do their jobs, and generally treated them with respect.

This management style fostered an environment of career growth and prosperity for employees. And, in turn, these companies grew and prospered as well.

Sure, there were times when I had a bad boss and dysfunction reigned supreme in my work environment, but they were rare—and those bad bosses didn't last long before they were shown the door.

I can say the same for some of the lousy clients I've had over the years... especially that first year or two when I started freelance copywriting. Some clients were keepers, and others definitely weren't.

I got most of my work via referrals, such as from former colleagues where I used to work, but often from others as well.

I had joined the local Washington, DC, chapter of the Direct Marketing Association—now part of the Association of National Advertisers (ANA)—when I first began freelancing. I used to attend monthly lunch events several times a year.

Someone at the chapter referred me to a company that published information in the emerging satellite communications and tech areas. I spoke with one of their marketing managers and took on some "magazine outer wrap" copywriting projects.

Because the company was less than a half hour away, I went in one day for a team meeting to kick off our first project together.

The copy I'd be working on was going to be used to promote a new magazine launch about the convergence of TV and online (which in hindsight didn't quite unfold the way people thought it would back in the late 1990s).

The team and I gathered around a long rectangular table in a nondescript conference room. We all chatted freely in a relaxed manner before the meeting began.

Then, when the silver-haired CEO entered the room and sat down at the head of the table, everyone immediately quieted and sat straight up. He was clearly in charge.

The CEO then started walking through a recent promotion that had been done in-house... and proceeded to rip it apart, page by page, component by component.

Like the worst dysfunctional family ever

Everyone around the conference room table visibly stiffened up even more. One by one, several of the employees were directly attacked by the CEO and their work ripped apart.

"Why did you leave so much white space there? Don't you know that's valuable real estate?" and other such criticisms came pouring out of the CEO's mouth.

It was like the worst imaginable dysfunctional family Thanksgiving dinner you've ever been to. The fear and anguish around the table were palpable. I almost forgot to breathe (but then I remembered, hey, I don't work here! Long exhale).

After a while, the CEO stopped his tirade long enough to notice me sitting off to his right at the table. "Who's this?" he demanded to know.

The marketing manager who had hired me said, "She's going to be writing the copy for the cover wrap."

The CEO seared his steely gaze on me. And in a commanding tone of voice, he ordered, "Make it sing!"

Not knowing what else to say, I sat up straight and replied, "Yes, sir!" I felt like I was responding to the U.S. Marines drill instructor in the movie *An Officer and a Gentleman*. I almost saluted him.

I got through that project without much hassle, fortunately, and did a few more, but then I didn't hear from them. And I was so busy with other, much better clients, it didn't matter.

So what happened to that company?

Less than two years later, the CEO sold the company's satellite TV publishing rights to a Canadian company—and fired just about all of his employees.

The moral of the story is, if you're getting treated badly by a client, chances are they're treating their employees pretty shabbily, too. And crap begets crap. People don't feel motivated to try hard, because no matter what they do, they get beaten down.

And risk-taking? *Fuhgeddaboudit.*

Savor and exercise your freedom

The lesson here is, there are plenty of client fish in the sea. You don't need to put up with this kind of stuff.

My experience was almost comical when I reflect back on it... but at the time, I WAS FREE... and these other folks weren't.

Cherish your freedom to choose who to work with, and who not to. Or know that you'll get through whatever nightmare project you're on, and then you'll MOVE ON.

Life is short—too short—to work with lousy clients. But almost everyone has a few bad ones along the way. It's part of the journey —and it's how you learn.

While I can't help you avoid all the "bad apples" out there, hopefully I've inspired you to be the "umpire of your life." I've given you ideas and tactics for how to improve your current situation substantially, no matter where you are now.

And I've got plenty more waiting for you in the chapters ahead.

In fact, this next chapter covers a topic that's crucial to the success of your freelance business. It's near and dear to copywriters' hearts.

I'm going to share with you some expertly honed strategies for making MORE money from your copywriting business.

Because let's face it—you're not doing this simply because you "love writing." This isn't a hobby… it's a *business*.

You need to make some serious coin from it. And you deserve to do so, especially when you're bringing value to the clients you serve.

The next chapter will show you how.

Chapter 6

Negotiating Secrets to Getting Paid More

(and Earning More R-E-S-P-E-C-T)

My great-grandmother was the ultimate "Tiger mom"... long before "Tiger mom-ing" was a thing.

Back in the early 1900s, her first-born son didn't get accepted into the US Naval Academy... despite his deceased father being a naval war hero (he was the officer on deck of the Battleship Maine when it blew up in Havana harbor).

In any case, my great-grandmother wasn't having any of it.

Ostensibly, her first-born son had been rejected due to a new minimum height requirement for incoming freshmen.

He was JUST borderline "too short."

You know who else was just borderline "too short"?

President Teddy Roosevelt... the commander-in-chief of the U.S. Military... and the former Assistant Secretary of the Navy.

So my great-grandmother arranged a face-to-face meeting with President Roosevelt (which she was able to do so in part since her husband—my great-grandfather—had played such an important role on the Battleship Maine).

And she confronted him about her son's rejection.

As family folklore has it, she told President Roosevelt to, "Stand up!"

He looked at her, sitting behind his desk, bewildered.

She repeated herself: "Stand up!"

Still, Roosevelt didn't quite understand.

Finally, in exasperation, she said more loudly and insistently, *"Stand UP!"*

This time, he got it... Roosevelt realized he himself wouldn't be able to meet the Naval Academy's new minimum height requirement.

He stamped the rejection letter she'd pushed towards him "Approved!" and her first-born son got into the U.S. Naval Academy... and her second-born son (my grandfather), also!

So now, I'm going to be your "tiger mom" and tell you to fight for what you want.

Want more (or better) clients? Want to charge higher fees? Want to put an end to the "feast or famine" rollercoaster?

Then get better at asking for what you want! Especially if you're a woman.

A recent study found that female freelancers get paid on average a *third* less than their male colleagues.

The study didn't just look at copywriters... I'm sure they made up a tiny sliver. It included everyone, from freelance photographers to musicians to event planners.

While I've known many a fellow female freelancer who I felt was undercharging for her services, I've also known many who charge a pretty penny—and get it.

(You can count this gal as one of them.)

So not all women stink at negotiating. And just because you're a guy doesn't mean you're great at it, either.

But the truth is, most people can be better at it—and get paid more than they're making now.

It all starts with this first initial step...

Overcome your fears and ask for what you're worth

If a potential new client seems overly concerned about what you're charging right from the get-go, that's a huge red flag.

They either don't value copy or they don't value you. Or likely BOTH.

And it may be best to simply run in the other direction—and leave yourself open for something better to come along.

The ideal scenario is to have someone come to you "pre-sold" on hiring you. And the best way is for this to happen organically via a recommendation from a colleague or past client.

The way to do this is to establish and maintain a broad referral network. Let any past work colleagues know what you're doing, and ask them to recommend you. (I talked about this in Chapter 2.)

When I left my Executive Marketing Director position at Phillips Publishing before going freelance, the majority of my copywriting clients the next few years came almost exclusively from past colleagues recommending me.

There was very little back and forth about what I wanted to charge. I either had researched the going rate for various projects by talking with other freelancers, or knew what we were paying freelance copywriters at Phillips for similar jobs.

So I would say, "Here's my fee" and that was that. *Hired!*

If someone comes to you referred by someone else, they are much more likely to want to hire you off the bat than a "cold" lead.

The lesson here is don't be shy about your fee.

Don't let them wear you down. (If they try too hard, walk away.)

And if you want to earn more money from copywriting, one of the fastest and easiest ways to do so is to raise your rates if they're too low. That's because…

It's probably time to give yourself a well-deserved "raise"!

Chances are you're overdue for a "raise" if you meet any or all of the following criteria:

- You've gained more experience writing copy and are getting better results.
- You've been working with more clients, including big names in your niche.
- You've recently written successful emails, lead tests, upsells, or sales pages or other promos and now have more impressive samples to show potential clients.

When you're a freelancer, the ball is in your court as far as how much you earn. It's not like working for a company where you sit down once a year with your boss for your performance review and are awarded an annual salary increase.

You have to do this for yourself! You're out in the savannah now, baby.

Figure out where you fall compared to what others are charging for similar projects. You can do so by talking to other copywriters and finding out what they charge.

Use "inside information" to your negotiating advantage

I did this many years ago before quoting one of my first direct mail packages to a client. The person was a friend at about the same level I was at the time. And they had recently done a similar project for the same client.

So I found out what they charged for their fee plus royalty and quoted the same. I put aside any fears that it was too much and put that price out there... even though it was three times what I had charged for a similar project previously. And I got the job!

Another way to research what others are charging is to check out as many copywriter websites as you can find that have a "rate sheet" displayed. Perhaps do a Google search on "copywriter for hire" or within a particular niche or type of copy (e.g. "supplement copywriter" or "email copywriter").

Now, I do NOT recommend you include a rate sheet on your own website. That's because it attracts price shoppers and it's best to customize a quote based on the proposed project, anyway.

But you can use this tactic to gauge what others are charging—and then set your rates accordingly.

There are some copywriter surveys out there that can also be useful. The founders of the popular Facebook group, The Copywriter Club, do an annual survey of freelance copywriters to find out what they're making. If you participate, you get to see the results!

And several years ago, copywriter and freelancer coach Abbey Woodcock did a survey of freelance copywriter earnings. Shockingly, she found that female copywriters were making 53 cents on the dollar compared to male copywriters... barely *HALF* as much!

That's even worse than that freelancer study I mentioned earlier. So if you're a woman, you may want to consider DOUBLING your rates.

How to raise your rates knowing clients will say "yes" to them

I talked about how to tell if it's time to raise your rates. But how can you confidently do so, knowing that clients will likely say "yes" to them?

That's often the biggest fear that holds copywriters back from raising their rates… whether it's with new clients they want to bring on, or with existing clients that they KNOW they've been undercharging for way too long, but don't know how to stop.

Aside from researching what the going rates are, and what particular clients typically pay for copy (since that can vary), I'm going to share a few sure-fire signs that you're in a great position to hike your fees.

If the clients you're working with now won't pay these higher rates, if you've got any of these other advantages going for you, chances are good you'll be able to show them the door without worrying about replacing them with a better, higher-paying client:

1. **You've got more clients than you have slots available.** When you start getting yourself booked out 3 to 6 months with clients on your "wait list" (and who have already plunked down a full 50% deposit to hold your time —you are doing that, right?) then it's pretty obvious you're now in demand. It's time to bump up your fees, maybe by a LOT.

2. **You've gotten a control or written a successful promo** for a client, and they want to hire you for another promo. You're sitting in the "catbird" seat here… especially if you gave them a deal to start. This is when you come back with a higher fee, and/or a royalty (or bigger royalty percentage), because you've shown them you're worth it.

3. **You've got at least a few controls or successful promos under your belt** with other clients, which you can now use as proof of your copywriting abilities for potential new clients. Know that this gives you a substantial edge over other copywriters to a publisher, supplement company, e-commerce company, or other business. Make sure your fees and incentives match the fact that you're now a "proven" copywriter.

4. **You haven't raised your fees in a loooooong time.** Maybe you're humming along, booked with steady clients,

making good money, and all seems fine. But even then, take a look around you. Did you happen to notice, as Mick Jagger put it in Shattered, the price of everything is going "up, up, up, up, UP!!!"

If for no other reason than mere inflation, maybe it's time to raise your rates. Not long ago, I went to my local dry cleaners, and noticed they had posted a sign in the last week showing their new pricing. You can do the same thing.

In fact, the start of a new year is a great time to raise your rates. Give your existing clients advance notice a few months beforehand and give them the opportunity to book your time at your existing rates—before they go up (and collect those 50% advances!) It's a logical time to increase your fees... just like all those businesses that do the same.

Now let's say you've decided it's time to give yourself a raise. And you've determined you're in a good position to do so ("imposter syndrome" aside... we'll get into that later).

How the heck do you quote with confidence... and CLOSE the deal?

Quoting with confidence is something many of us struggle with. Okay, pretty much ALL of us struggle with it.

But trust me—it gets easier the more often you do it.

It may sound crazy, but practice saying your (new) quote out loud. Say it enough times that it flows out of you naturally, without hesitation.

Do NOT be tempted to go in with a lower number... always aim a bit higher. You can always adjust from there. But it's best to pick a firm number and stay with it.

If you think the client is eager or pre-sold (i.e. via a strong referral) on hiring you, just put that seemingly "ballsy" number out there.

You'll be surprised how the vast majority of the time the response is simply, "Okay", with no pushback.

Or you can give a range if the potential client is one that you're not as confident about closing. Just make sure the number on the low end is one you'd be satisfied with, because they will hang on to that bottom-of-the-range figure like a dog with a bone.

This also leaves the door open for adding in fees for other things, such as emails or other ancillary copy in addition to sales page or VSL copy, or a second headline/lead test version, in order to boost your fee to the higher end of that range (or beyond).

Plus, there are incentives you can negotiate like a one-time bonus for, say, getting the control... an ongoing royalty... and/or a revenue share deal. I've had clients not want to pay the copywriting fee I quote for a long-form promo, for example (the fee is in addition to ongoing royalties if it becomes a control).

So I'll take the additional amount that they say is over their "budget" and turn that into a one-time bonus that they pay me if my promo becomes their new control. This is in addition to royalties. That way I can still get my full fee (and pretty much always do!)

I've also built in incentives for writing email copy. For example, I charged a flat fee to write three new emails or "lifts" driving traffic to a sales page for one client... with the stipulation that I'd get a one-time bonus of the entire flat fee if one of my emails became their new control email. One of them became the new control, and I got *double* my fee!

It's important to make sure you outline in your contract that the client will provide reports showing the actual royalties or other incentives due (when I was writing mostly direct mail, I'd require copies of the actual postage receipts showing the mailing totals).

Now, the truth is, a lot of this comes down to the trust factor you have with the client. If it's someone you haven't worked with before, do you know copywriters who've done similar royalty deals with them? If so, talk to them and find out how good the client is about following through with the payments. It may be an eye-opening conversation.

The bottom line is to keep in mind the following...

Charging higher fees instantly elevates you

Always keep in mind that if your fee is too low compared to the going rate, you may raise doubts or concerns in your prospective client's mind that you're not as good at what you do.

I've seen many talented copywriters and designers who are guilty of undercharging for their services compared to market rates. As I've mentioned before, they're often women.

For example, one top male graphic designer I know charges twice what other experienced designers charge—and he's always booked out months in advance.

But men don't always out-do women in this department. A male copywriter I met once at a big direct marketing event had a huge spread of magalogs he'd written out on display at his table in the exhibit hall.

Upon further discussion, we realized we worked with some of the same clients.

And though I didn't divulge this to him, I was getting paid at least two-thirds more than him for writing magalogs—plus earning substantial royalties.

In fact, my jaw just about dropped to the ground when he told me he wasn't charging royalties. Yikes!

What to do if you're starting out or NOT sitting in the "catbird seat"

What if you're just starting out? How do you quote with confidence when you're hungry for those first initial clients... or you just lost a major client who was providing the bulk of your income, and you're worrying about landing new business so you can pay the bills?

Whatever you do, don't accept whatever fee or project terms the client offers. Stay in the driver's seat.

And remember: clients can smell desperation a mile away… so don't even hint at it!

It's just like that cheetah analogy in the Introduction. If they think you're "easy prey", you're done.

Sure, if you're just starting out, you're hungry. But if you come across as desperate, you're setting yourself up to attract the bottom-feeders of clients who will often take advantage of you… without it leading to something better, even if they promise it will.

And if you've found yourself losing one of your main income sources, this is the time to reach out to past clients and work your network of other copywriters, potential clients on your radars, people you consider mentors, and others.

Position it as a positive: you've reached a point with your client where they're happy with how their business is growing and this has freed you up to take on a *limited* number of new clients that meet your criteria (sound like you're being selective, not desperate, and build a little scarcity/urgency in).

Use your powers of persuasion to get what you want

No matter what situation you're in: "hungry" to bring on a new client, or "well-fed" but always looking for good clients to add to your roster, it's best to get on a Zoom or phone call and close that client, using techniques honed by the savviest sales closers.

And often, the best sales closers know not only how to overcome your biggest objections (dealing with the logical side of the brain), they know how to zero in on your biggest pain points (dealing with the emotional side of the brain… the side where the vast majority of purchase decisions are made).

Chances are you've had your own experiences with salespeople who've convinced you to spend money with them... whether it's a timeshare you now regret owning... a pair of shoes you could have gotten for much less somewhere else... or the lifetime package of kickboxing classes you tired of after the first few months (been there, done that!)

Or perhaps you recall using your powers of persuasion to convince someone to give you what you want... say, a second attempt asking someone to dance (like my husband did that night we first met) or persuading a boss to give you a much-deserved pay raise.

While you can (and should) read and study sales-closing techniques from legendary experts like Dale Carnegie or Zig Ziglar, you should also draw on your own personal experiences with what works.

Hit their biggest pain points, and the world is your oyster

I remember when I was a few years out of college working in the actuarial department of a large insurance company (I have a Bachelor's degree in mathematics and statistics).

I decided I wanted to start taking classes part time at night to earn a Master of Business Administration (MBA) degree in Marketing. And I wanted to take advantage of the company's tuition reimbursement program to help pay for it.

In order to get tuition reimbursement, my boss' boss—"Mr. Sirian" —had to approve it. (Back then, bosses were often referred to with this level of formality). And to get his approval, I had to have a meeting with him and make my case for it.

I was in my early 20s and single at the time, and Mr. Sirian was only seven or eight years older than me. I knew he was pursuing his MBA part-time at night at the same college to which I'd been admitted. I also knew that he was married, with two young children.

We sat down at a table in his large window office, and I answered his questions about why I wanted to pursue my MBA. Then, after making what I felt was a strong case, Mr. Sirian decided to challenge me with the following question:

"You're only in your early twenties and have been out of college just a few years. Don't you think you should wait and get more work experience before pursuing your MBA?"

This was the moment where I knew exactly how to respond. And I pounced.

I looked Mr. Sirian in the eye and said, "The way I see it, it'll be much easier for me to earn my MBA part-time now while I'm still single and don't have kids, rather than try to juggle it later when I'm married with a family."

Mr. Sirian stared back at me, with a faint hint of exhaustion in his eyes, as if suffering from a chronic lack of sleep. He could NOT meet my answer with a counterargument.

I saw his pain point... and I honed right in on it. Mr. Sirian approved the several thousand dollars' worth of company-paid tuition reimbursement right then and there.

And I went on to complete my MBA degree part-time in addition to working my full-time job, getting it out of the way before I got married and started a family.

I've used the same "biggest pain point" approach to close high-paying consulting or copy chiefing deals.

When dealing with these bigger types of deals, be careful not to give away the "store"... but do come prepared having done your research and knowing what areas the client has the biggest need for your services—and give them a sampling of how you can help.

Then don't be afraid to push them to make a decision by building in urgency (you can't hold that time in your schedule indefinitely)... or better yet, zeroing in on what you know is their biggest pain point.

The secret is to listen and ask questions more than you talk in these crucial client conversations, because that's how you'll discover how you'll be able to close them.

And they won't be able to send that big fat advance payment over to you fast enough!

The #1 secret to getting paid more

The biggest differentiator for negotiating better-paying deals and attracting higher-quality clients is this simple fact: the highest-paid earners are often the top performers.

This is one of the things I love most about being a direct response copywriter. Results are almost always 100% measurable and traceable back to your efforts.

That means—as long as you have the "ballsiness" to ask for what you're worth—it's an even playing field.

(I'm not dismissing that there is discrimination that can act as a barrier, and that needs to change … but most good clients are only going to care about whether you can get them results.)

More than just about any other career field, your earning potential as a freelance copywriter is based on merit.

It's not based on who you brown-nose or who you talk over in a meeting or whose ideas you take credit for or other things that happen all too often in the corporate world. (Trust me, I've seen all of it!)

And that means your very best strategy to getting paid more… besides developing your client "badassery" skills… is to get REALLY good at what you do.

One way to shorten your climb to the top is to learn all you can from those who've actually DONE it themselves. Back when I was starting out, I couldn't find a single A-lister who was teaching folks how to write copy via courses or mentoring.

On occasion, though, I could get a much more experienced copywriter to look at my copy. This helped me tremendously early on and greatly accelerated my career.

And now I'm helping other copywriters do the same. In recent years, I've offered group mentoring programs and "sprints." I've also created several best-in-class trainings.

Check out the Wrap-up chapter at the end of this book for more details plus other valuable resources that can help you get "dangerously good" at writing copy—and working with clients.

But for now, let's zero in on what you need to run your freelance business like a badass…

Chapter 7

Zero Jerk Tolerance: Running Your Freelance Business Like a Badass

F reelance copywriting often seems more challenging than ever these days.

Between the gazillions of copywriters you're competing with, and the advent of ChatGPT and more sophisticated AI tools coming out each day, it may seem like it's harder than ever to launch and maintain a successful freelance career.

But the truth is, there's still plenty of opportunity to succeed as a copywriter. You just need to zero in on the right things.

I've talked about how important it is to focus on honing your copywriting skills so you can consistently deliver successful, winning copy when you work with clients.

Being great at writing copy is essential to going far in this freelance copywriting biz, for sure.

But do you know what's even more important?

The right *mindset*.

The #1 skill for handling clients like a boss

Now, how can mindset be even MORE important than being great at writing copy?

Because I've personally witnessed great copywriters who sucked when it came to standing up for themselves... who were unable to ask for the pay they deserved... and who tolerated bad client behavior when they had so many other options.

Meanwhile, I've seen others who weren't as good at writing copy sail right by them because they had the confidence to cut higher-paying deals or shut down bad behavior.

So where does one get this confidence, I'm so often asked?

It comes from mastering this #1 skill for handling clients like a boss: setting boundaries.

Setting boundaries can save you a heap of trouble when it comes to dealing with clients. I'm talking about things like...

- **Not jumping when the client says "jump"**—i.e. feeling you have to say "yes" to everything, including unreasonable requests... which then leads to even more unreasonable requests...
- Taking the quote you're about to give a client and **increasing it by 50% or even doubling it**, then putting it out there even though you're terrified to do so...
- **Shutting down bad client behavior** the first time it rears its ugly head (and still being able to have a good and profitable long-term working relationship, assuming you want to...)
- **Spelling out deliverables clearly** and fending off "scope creep" at the onset by never giving away anything for "free"...
- **Always getting paid an advance** (usually 50%) upfront before doing a lick of work... even with clients you've

worked with before, because priorities can change and YOU don't want to be left holding the bag...

- And **countless more client-management tactics** that help you run your freelance biz more smoothly.

Do these things and an amazing thing starts to happen...

You start to develop greater confidence!

This confidence grows from staying true to what YOU need to get out of the client relationship.

It grows from valuing and respecting yourself enough to speak up or push back when needed.

And it grows from how clients start to treat you once you begin setting boundaries and valuing yourself.

That's because when you stand up for yourself in a professional and confident way, clients respect you more right from the get-go... and they're much less likely to try any of that stupid stuff or make unreasonable requests as a result.

So you can more easily negotiate higher pay, better terms, and avoid client "BS."

And you know what else? They may even respect the copy you produce even more.

I mean, you still have to write good copy... but if a client is biased towards not fully respecting you as a professional, they will look more for where your copy is failing or coming up short.

But when they respect you more as a professional, the opposite is true.

I'm hoping this inspires you to look at your entire client management process in total... i.e., how you do all the following things:

- Respond to potential clients and close them.
- The quotes, time frames, and payment terms you provide in proposals.
- Your contracts and agreements: how "airtight" are they?
- Your process for working with a client from start to finish.
- Client follow-up during the project to get feedback and wrap things up.
- Invoicing and getting paid (and any ongoing compensation like royalties).
- Getting another future project if it all went well and/or a testimonial or referral.

Are there any "holes" in any of these areas of your freelance business that setting stronger boundaries could help with?

Taking the time to examine all of these areas and fixing what's broken will set you up for far greater success in your freelance business.

Bonus: Being able to set boundaries and knowing what works for you —and what doesn't, and being confident enough to ask for what you want, will help you in other areas of your life as well!

The perils of being a people pleaser

Let's talk about that topic a bit more... because it's often the most difficult skill for many of us to master. Perhaps standing up for yourself and calling out bad behavior feels "wrong" to you.

Maybe you weren't allowed to do that for yourself when you were young... or for various reasons developed people-pleasing tendencies, like so many of us.

Many freelancers tend towards this kind of people-pleasing mode when dealing with clients. Heck, many employees do it with their bosses. Yet it can really get in the way when it comes to enforcing reasonable boundaries.

We've all run into situations with a client or someone else who does something that's out of line. I've already shared some stories from my own awkward moments I've encountered throughout my career and how I handled them—and there's more of them.

But here's the thing... when this kind of bad behavior happens, you HAVE to call it out. Especially when it's within a client relationship or in the workplace. And the sooner you do so, the better.

Because otherwise that "jerk" will feel like they can walk all over you. And they'll do it. Again and again and again.

That's why it's crucial to develop and enforce a "Zero Jerk Tolerance" policy when it comes to your freelancing, business, or other professional life.

Having been in this freelance copywriting game long enough that I'm probably "unemployable," you can bet I've seen my share of good clients and oh-so-bad clients along the way.

As I got better at copywriting and developed a track record of successful promos and beating controls written by legends like Jim Rutz and Parris Lampropoulos, I had less of the client "bottom feeders" to deal with.

But even when you're up near the top of the food chain, you'd be amazed how many near-client disasters I've had to nimbly avoid... or how many times I had to stick firmly to my guns when asked for something I wasn't willing to bend on.

It still feels like it wasn't that long ago (although it was) that I was eagerly accepting whatever work I could and worrying that maybe I was charging too much or too little.

That sweaty-handed "fear factor" never really goes away

But here's the thing. When you decide to arm yourself with knowledge and become aware of the games clients play... and discover how to navigate those shark-filled waters, things start to go more smoothly.

As I said before, you'll likely start to feel much more confident. The result?

You'll find clients not only respect you more, they'll start to bend to your will. And your earnings and passive income potential start to soar.

This is where learning how to apply your client "badassery" can really come in handy.

The first step is to avoid making this common mistake…

Stop being a pushover and set boundaries with your clients

One common pain point I've heard time and again was voiced recently by a copywriter I met. She said, "I feel like I'm always saying 'yes' to things, and am too eager to please."

I'm sure many other copywriters—both male and female—can relate to this, too.

Many times, in the excitement of earning freelance income for the first time and closing new clients, you may overstretch yourself by saying "yes" to too many projects.

Then you find yourself working *waaaaaay* more hours than you want, feeling constantly stressed, and worrying about the quality of your work.

And you should worry, because if you take on too much work at once, you usually won't be able to do as good a job for your clients… and you may end up burning bridges.

It's much better to take on a manageable load and then be able to do your best possible work… which will lead to more work from that client, maybe even referrals to other clients, and some "wins" that will open even more doors for you.

Here's something else: when you start saying "no" to things like a last-minute rush project or if you can squeeze something in... and offer up a later slot instead that fits within a more reasonable schedule, those clients respect you more.

They think, "Wow, this person is pretty booked up... they must be GOOD," and suddenly the power balance falls more into your hands, not theirs.

Plus, you may be able to negotiate higher fees... and know you'll be able to do a better job without sacrificing your sanity, which will pay off in the long run.

So don't be afraid to push back, stand up for yourself, and be a bit of a badass... clients will respect you more for it.

You're going to need that backbone, because there are plenty of instances where it will come in handy. Especially when you come face-to-face with what I cover in the next chapter...

Chapter 8

The 3 Big Lies Clients Tell Copywriters... and How to Call "BS" on Them

As you travel along your freelance journey, you can bet you'll hear at least one of the three big lies clients tell copywriters, which I'll reveal in just a moment.

Hopefully, armed with the knowledge I've given you so far, you'll be able to avoid being victimized by them.

Some of these big lies I've already covered in the chapter about the 7 types of clients you meet on the road to copywriting "hell." So they shouldn't shock you.

Let's start with…

The biggest, baddest, most "Godzilla-like" client lie

Big Client Lie #1: "We're only going to need XYZ from you"

Let's say you find out what a client says they need from you and give them a quote that's accepted.

You "shake hands" on the deal, get everything else in order, and clear your schedule to start work.

Then suddenly the client's "plan" is changing. Now it's five emails they need ("can you just throw in three more?") or "can you also do a short landing page and include that in what you quoted?"

Hellz no!

"Scope creep" is real, my friend, just like those giant alligators that periodically crawl out of one of the 5 billion+ ponds in Florida and are big enough to eat a horse!

If you see that "Godzilla" alligator coming at you, either run in the other direction (especially if it really is an alligator), or stand your ground. Here's how you do the latter.

Say it with me: "That's outside the scope of our agreement. I'm happy to work that in (assuming you have time), but I'm going to need to charge you additional for that."

End of story. Now here's a similar client lie you may find yourself a victim of...

When it's *still* not final until after the "fat lady" sings her 100th song

Big Client Lie #2: "That's the final launch plan"

Sometimes you start working with a client. You're told the launch plan is now final, and it's time to write the copy (usually under an insane deadline).

You find out all the details on the offer, the upsells, the different email sequences and what they're selling.

Then you start fleshing out your wonderful, beautiful copy... only to experience the kind of fresh hell that will drive you mad!

It happens when you hear your client say...

"Oh, we changed the upsell and now we're doing this instead," or, "We decided to offer something different in the welcome emails," or, "we now want to cover this in video #2"...

...or something horrific along those lines.

And you realize that launch "plan" was nothing more than an illusion. They're simply flying by the seat of their pants—and no one can make a decision and stick with it.

I once experienced this on a launch project years ago with a well-known "guru" who was a dream to work with. EXCEPT... someone else kept feeding him competing advice, causing him to constantly change his video script strategy or upsells or other aspects of the launch.

That's when I resorted to something I call "Just in time" copywriting. It's loosely based on a manufacturing technique the Japanese came up with that I learned about when I was getting my MBA degree.

I would simply wait until the VERY last minute before the copy was due (this was relatively easy copy for me to write). And then, once I confirmed the plan hadn't changed in the last ten minutes, I'd write it just in time, and send it off! Your results with this will vary. This is when you have to let go of your perfectionistic tendencies and just get 'er done!

Now let's look at the third and sometimes most dangerous client lie...

Like marrying someone you just met in Vegas—but worse

Big Client Lie #3: "We'll pay you for your copy if we use it"

One thing I've never done in my freelance copywriting career is to write copy on "spec"... where you write a piece of copy, and the client decides if they like it and THEN pays you for it... rather than hiring you up-front like the true professional you are.

Yes, I'm a little biased against these kinds of deals, but I know for some people they have opened up doors that otherwise wouldn't have opened.

The thing is, you can't just take their word upfront that they're going to pay you later.

Doing work on "spec" before nailing down all the details is like marrying someone you just met in Vegas—and to make matters worse, without a pre-nuptial agreement.

It's essential you agree to all the terms, especially how much and on what basis you'll get paid if the client uses your copy.

Otherwise, as soon as you turn in that copy you've poured your blood, sweat, and tears into, you've lost all of your negotiating leverage.

How to keep "spec" from being a 4-letter word

My advice when you're just getting started as a freelance copywriter is to take on as many "starter" projects as possible and get paid to learn.

Don't worry about "niching" at this point... take a wide variety of projects so you can get in your "reps," earn money, and get some samples.

Gaining experience with a wide range of products will help you develop faster as well, and become more flexible, creative, and adaptable.

But if you feel you need to do a copywriting project on "spec" to get your foot in the door with your dream client or niche, or because you don't have any samples just yet, here's what I suggest you do.

First off, as I mentioned earlier, make sure you outline all the specifics of your spec assignment BEFORE you agree to do it.

If it's a sales email you're writing, nail down exactly how much you'll get paid and when, and on what basis.

For example, maybe you'll write it for free, and if they test it and it becomes their new control email, they'll pay you a pre-determined fee for it.

Just be aware that when you offer to write copy for free, clients won't value you.

That's why I suggest re-framing it... maybe something like: "If I write this email for you to drive traffic to your sales page and it generates at least one sale, you'll pay me $100. Otherwise, you owe me nothing."

Then you're talking about what the client cares about—getting results—and shows that you're confident your work will deliver.

Obviously try to get as high as a fee as possible… after all, the client isn't risking anything up front, YOU are in terms of your time, effort, and opportunity costs.

If the client can get a winning email out of the deal that drives more traffic to their promotions and generates higher revenue, that's MONEY for them… and it should mean money for you, too. You've earned it!

Secrets to negotiating royalties or bonuses on your "spec" project

You may be able to negotiate an even better deal by writing a new headline and lead on spec. Let's say a client has a sales page that's been doing well, but is starting to fatigue as all promos eventually do.

Rather than start over from scratch and hire a copywriter to write a whole new promo, they may have you do a headline and lead test to see if they can get themselves a "new" control.

Note: Whenever I have a royalty-paying control sales page, I do this at no cost for my clients as needed, since it's in my interest to keep it a strong performer. It's one of the advantages for clients of doing royalty deals that create a "win/win" partnership.

Now, writing a new headline and lead takes a lot more time than it looks. You have to dive in and do the research and get up to speed on the avatar, the product, the market, and the other messaging that's out there so you can come up with something new yet relevant to say... a brand-new angle.

That's why it's only fair that if you write a headline/lead on spec, the client has some skin in the game as well if they decide to test it.

I recommend you put together an arrangement where the client pays you a fee—let's say $500 to $1,000—if they like your headline/lead and, with or without some additional edits on your part, they decide to test it.

Then work in a performance bonus. If they test your new headline/lead and it beats their current control, have them pay you another $500 to $2,000 (or as high as you're able to get) one-time performance bonus.

Negotiating royalties on a headline/lead test may be difficult, as the client may already be paying them to whoever wrote the entire sales page promo.

But in many cases, clients may be open to paying you a royalty (typically for just the headline/lead, you may be able to get 1-2% of sales), so you may want that to be your "going in" position, with the one-time performance bonus as your "back-up."

And put ALL of this in writing before you do a lick of work... with your signature and, more importantly, the signature of someone in a position of authority at your client's company on the dotted line.

When it MIGHT make sense to take on a spec project (maybe)

I generally despise the whole concept of spec assignments, but like I said, in some cases, they can help.

For one of my mentees, it landed him a project with royalty potential with one of the major publishers he'd been yearning to work with.

But a better way in may be to consider becoming an in-house employee at one of those major direct marketing companies (keeping in mind the pros and cons I outline in Chapter 11).

I never would have had the success I've had (or even known about copywriting) if I hadn't spent six years at Phillips Publishing first.

Aside from the knowledge I gained, those connections and resulting referrals I mentioned earlier have helped keep me swimming in work ever since.

But I always made sure I kept doing this next step, even when I had clients booked in advance for a year out or more.

Just like when cheetahs on the savannah slack off on hunting prey—or impalas let down their guard—you, too, could end up starving or become someone's next meal if you get too comfortable.

Let's say you've got a sweet gig working full-time on retainer with primarily one client. When you put all your eggs in one basket, and something happens to that basket (it always does), you may find yourself "scrambling" to line up work fast.

It's why legendary direct response marketer and copywriter Dan Kennedy says, "The most dangerous number in business is ONE."

So no matter what your situation or how good you have it right now, you want to follow this rule:

Always. Be. Prospecting!

Yes, that means even if you've already got a sweet retainer arrangement (or two) or are working in-house. Nothing lasts forever, baby!

I get my hair done by a stylist who has her own "solo" salon in a complex of other solo salons. It's near where I live outside Washington, DC.

She's told me before about a stylist who works out of a solo salon down the hall from her, when he's not flying out to LA to do Jennifer Lopez's or Kim Kardashian's hair... or taking the train to New York for modeling shoots.

I recently asked her if he was taking on new clients (since someone I knew was curious). I assumed the answer would be "no" based on his star-studded clientele.

But my stylist told me *of course* he was... they all learned in hair school that you always put one day aside a week for new client appointments.

That's because no matter how high up you are, there is always turnover. You want to be prepared and always have a "wait list" of clients on reserve.

So consider putting one day aside a week (or a similar amount) for new client development... and keep adding to that potential "wait list" (a.k.a. "back-up plan").

In the next chapter, I'll share with you how I recommend you run your freelance copywriting business with the hordes of paying clients you'll be bringing in as a result of your efforts (or already are bringing in).

These tactics will help keep the dough rolling in while saving you from needless hassle (you can thank me later!)

Chapter 9

My 3 Golden Rules for Lucrative, Hassle-Free Freelancing Bliss

O ne of the hardest things to do as a freelancer is to walk away when you should. Knowing when to say "BUH-bye" is a combination of know-how, experience, and pure and simple guts.

Ideally, this BUH-bye decision, when warranted, happens *before* a project even gets off the ground.

But that's not always the case.

Glaring red flags often get ignored in the blissful first-date-like throes of a new client-copywriter relationship.

You feel wanted, optimistic, and maybe a bit too hungry for the opportunity (and the $$).

But it's a jungle out there—take it from a long-time freelancer. There are more snakes in the grass and traps to avoid than ever before.

Obviously, not all companies and clients are bad to work with or devalue what we do. But there are some potential clients I avoid like the plague (see Chapter 4 for a list of the seven types that will make your life miserable). For those whose "red flags" aren't immediately visible, I screen them carefully... and make sure they're willing to work with me on my terms.

If I haven't convinced you by now, you need to have your own terms at the ready. For starters, make sure you've got your own contract. And if the client has their own contract and you use that instead, don't be afraid to ask them to change what's in it.

By doing so, you can steer clear of client landmines and enjoy a more lucrative, hassle-free freelance business. In short, the bliss we're all seeking as freelancers!

So even if you really need the money—and the opportunity—here are three golden rules for running your freelance business...

Show me the money!

Golden rule #1: Work NEVER begins until *after* your advance (typically 50% of your full copywriting fee) lands in your checking account free and clear.

Aside from an initial sales call with the client to discuss the project before booking your time, and firming up your agreement, you do nothing until the moolah—i.e. advance—is in your hot little hands.

No research. *No* brainstorming calls. *Not a single word* of copy (unless you can't help having an idea come to you in the middle of the night and you scribble it down).

Any and all deadlines you agree to must hinge on getting the advance within the time frame you request.

Once again, I require a 50% advance on copywriting projects. If the client is outside the US, I require 100% due to the hassle of chasing down non-payers of any remaining balance. And if it's copy chiefing or consulting services, I require 100% upfront... since unlike with copywriting projects, I can't keep them from using my work without full payment.

When invoicing (which I always recommend you do immediately once the client accepts your proposal), I allow 7-10 days for them to pay me and book a slot in my schedule.

But many times I get my advance within a day or two. It's pretty much always possible for clients to do this, even if they try blaming it on the accounting department. And there's things like ACH bank transfers, Wise for international payments, and PayPal to get paid in a speedy fashion if the project is one that they want you to start on ASAP.

You have to be FIRM on the "work begins after the advance is received" golden rule. I've seen way too many nightmare scenarios to count when an overly excited freelancer gets rolling right away without cold, hard cash in hand.

That's because sometimes the client's plans change to move forward with a project or new launch. Or their promotional schedule shifts and they don't need your copy for six months. Or the economy tanks or there's some major distracting event.

Or the supplier couldn't come through with the product. Or about 39,586 other things that could go wrong that have *nothing* to do with you and are out of your control.

Or maybe, the client simply turns out to be a jerk, which you begin to realize after a few interactions back and forth when they are unwilling to accommodate simple requests or won't agree to reasonable terms... or basically FAILS to treat you like a professional.

Meanwhile, if you've already started plugging away, trusting the client would hold up their end of the bargain, you've ended up doing work for free. To make matters worse, you've maybe even turned work away to do so... all of which costs you TIME and MONEY.

It's a purely one-sided situation that works against you if you start work before you've gotten paid your advance. So simply don't do it. EV-ah.

Here's another tactic for keeping client "BS" from wrecking your freelance life…

Cover your butt... and make 'em sign on the dotted line

Golden rule #2: Firm up your client agreement or contract in advance—and make sure it reflects your own interests as well as the client's.

Just like a prenuptial agreement, you should always ensure you have a contract in place with your client that's discussed and agreed to in advance, while you're still in that "honeymoon" period of the client relationship.

I will confess, though, that I was several years into freelance copywriting before I started using my own detailed copywriting agreement with clients.

Up until that time, I used an "invoice/contract" that had the basics on it: the advance, the balance, what copy I'd be writing, payment terms, and the details of any royalty or bonus arrangement. I'd then have the client sign and return it to me.

But along the way, I realized I needed an agreement that would protect my interests in the oddball event that a project I had started on would get "killed" or cancelled.

This is something that can happen for some of the same reasons as cited above (it's not always because the client is dissatisfied).

And even though I can count on less than one hand how many times I'd had a project killed or cancelled over the past few decades, I felt it was worth spelling out.

Plus, I had other things that needed to be spelled out, like what would happen if the copy was used for something else (say converted into a sales page or VSL or direct mail promo) and it was a royalty arrangement.

True story: A copywriter friend of mine wrote an incredibly successful direct mail promo for a major financial publisher. It mailed to millions of names and earned her a huge amount in well-deserved royalties. It was considered one of the company's best-performing promos of all time.

Then the company started doing something that was fairly new at the time: they converted her direct mail promo into an online sales page (this was many years ago). And it did gangbusters online, too!

Except my friend didn't get a penny of royalties from it… because she had only spelled out royalties generated from direct mail use of her promo copy, NOT online as well.

That's why no matter how much a client swears they'll never use my promo in direct mail OR online, I always specify royalties both ways… and for other types of uses.

But back to my newfound awareness of my need for an actual, grown-up contract. I also realized I wasn't covering my butt in the event of any legal or compliance issues.

Even though I always make my agreements between my S-Corp company name (you should do the same if you have an S-Corp or LLC) and the client's, which would provide some protection, I wanted to make sure I wasn't on the hook for things that should be the client's responsibility.

After all, they're getting the vast majority of the revenue. And there are several things you lose control of as a copywriter once you turn in the copy.

Of course, if it's a big company you're working with, they likely have their own contract… which an army of lawyers has carefully crafted to 100% favor *their* client's interests and not yours.

But that doesn't mean you can't negotiate or change terms that you don't like. Everything's negotiable.

That's why you want to go through the client's contract carefully before you sign it. Decide what you can live with and if there's anything you want to push back on.

(If it's your first big-company contract, consider hiring a lawyer to review it with you. Doing this once can be a valuable educational experience that's worth the expense.)

And definitely make sure you use your own contract (I like calling it a "copywriting agreement" since it's less threatening) when you work with clients who don't have one.

Just send it over along with your invoice for that 50% advance, and have them sign and return it to you.

I guarantee having all these particulars spelled-out *ahead* of time will save you a world of frustration and pain (and hard-earned money, too!) As will following this next rule...

If it doesn't work for you, it's a no-go!

Golden rule #3: YOU provide the quotes and estimates for your work... *not* the client!

Could you imagine talking with a contractor to remodel your kitchen or hiring an accountant to do your taxes, and YOU telling them exactly what you're going to pay them for the work?

Of course not! You might mention what your budget is, of course, but it's not up to you to determine the pricing.

You can take or leave what they offer to do the work for... but you have to trust that the contractor and accountant have a much better understanding of the actual costs and value of what they do.

And you're free to get multiple quotes, but it's not always a "lowest cost" decision. You look at their experience, recommendations, and other factors.

The same is true for copywriting, of course.

Beware of potential clients who try to dictate THEIR "fee schedule" on you, as if it's a one-size-fits-all kind of thing.

Sure, they may have their budgets... and maybe they can't afford you. Maybe you're willing to come down a bit for an initial project (and perhaps you can structure a deal with a one-time bonus, like I mentioned in Chapter 6).

But the point is, there are many ways to make working together a "win/win" arrangement.

Clients who only want it to be one-sided, and want to treat you like another interchangeable cog in the machine, are probably ones that won't treat you any better down the road, no matter how well your copy performs for them.

That's because they don't value what GOOD copy can do for their business.

The most successful direct response companies on the planet and throughout recent history have all been willing to pay for good copy. More importantly, they've been willing to richly reward those unicorn-like writers who can bring them those huge winners.

But there are plenty of small, growing companies who also place a high premium on copy that can convert in an increasingly competitive marketplace.

Now that you know these three "golden rules" of running your freelance business, I hope they save you future headaches, hassles, and bad client nightmares going forward.

I also hope they help propel you to the next level of your freelance business: the copywriting big time! So turn the page and keep reading so you can get yourself there far faster.

Chapter 10

How to Break into the Copywriting "Big Time" and Start Racking Up Big Fees and Royalties

A freelance copywriter once wrote to me with a question I hear often.

It's one I've addressed in podcasts I've been interviewed on, or when I've appeared on stage at copywriting events.

Here's his question:

"How possible is it for someone with no prior connection or copy mentor, etc. to get an opportunity to write for the types of clients you and other top-name copywriters write for?

"Is it a bit of a closed-shop (for want of a better phrase)? Or is there a way that an 'unknown' can (from a cold start) properly come to the attention of the right people and get an opportunity to work on an initial project to prove themselves?

"If I get any response at all from the major health publishers, it has been along the lines of 'we're not looking for any other copywriters at present' (which seems to run contrary to what I hear some saying online or in interviews that the major publishers/supplement companies are always looking for the talented copywriters that they don't yet know about)."

It's true that many major direct response companies are dying to bring on more copywriters to help them out. It's also true that it's hard to break in.

When I was starting out as a freelance copywriter more than a few decades ago, I had already racked up several years of marketing experience with Phillips Publishing, one of the biggest direct response companies at the time. (The company was since broken up into various subsidiaries and sold several years ago.)

So I had a lot of valuable connections. And because I had already developed a reputation as a good copywriter while I was at Phillips, I often got referred to clients by someone who knew me, usually past colleagues.

But I still had to climb the "copywriting ladder" so I could break into the "big time" and start earning high fees and royalties. Here's how I did it...

Small projects lead to big things

Despite having run a successful supplement business and having had a good run at a major publisher, when I first started out as a freelance copywriter I worked on small, flat-fee projects (with no royalty potential like long-form copy).

These initial projects generally performed well... which opened the door for me to do bigger projects.

But even with a successful control or two under my belt for some smaller companies, the bigger guns weren't impressed. Despite reaching out to two major direct response companies I wanted to work with—my "dream" clients—they ignored me at first.

Then when I hit a "home run" for a major publisher at the time— and beat a control written by the legendary copywriter Jim Rutz (the *first* time—there was a second time, too), those two companies couldn't hire me fast enough.

So each step you take... each client you work with... see it as a stepladder taking you to that next level. Work hard to prove yourself each and every time, learn from your inevitable failures and mistakes, and constantly strive to get better at your craft.

How to give yourself your own "big break"

It can feel like successful copywriters appear overnight, with social media having us believe people go from zero to hero in the blink of an eye.

This mirage can—unfortunately—beat down the positive ambition in even the most optimistic of people.

The reality for most people is a more complex journey of learning how to get good at writing copy and "failing forward" toward success. This means you learn to accept, and even welcome, failure as a way of taking risks and learning from your mistakes.

But sometimes being afraid of failing, or seeing yourself as a failure, can keep you feeling stuck.

Perhaps you're just starting out in copywriting and consider yourself a "newbie"... or you're struggling to bring in as much income from copywriting as you'd like.

And even if you are bringing in solid earnings, you may feel you're still not charging enough for the value you deliver... or you wrestle with "imposter syndrome" and don't feel confident enough to ask for what you want from clients.

Either way, the constant noise of social media and various groups leaves you constantly comparing yourself to others and feeling like you're not keeping up.

So here's the truth: It's never an easy, straight path to the top. Or even halfway to the top. NEVER.

The journey you take requires constant focus and dedication to improving and getting better... and working on your mindset as well.

You have to set realistic expectations, and seize the opportunities that come along.

Most importantly, you must have a consistently applied work ethic and plan to get where you want to go.

The other thing you want to make sure you get good at is accepting and using feedback from clients, coaches, or mentors.

If you really, REALLY want to accelerate your climb up the copywriting ladder and ramp up the power of your copy...

Turn in first drafts that consistently wow your clients and smooth the path towards headache-free approval (and immediate re-bookings)...

And reap the rewards of being able to command higher fees and rake in fat royalties and bonuses that take your earnings to a whole new level...

You need to not just accept, but seek out honest (and, at times, brutally honest) feedback. That's right...

You need someone to rip the "band-aid" off your copy!

Back when I was a marketer running the Healthy Directions supplement business when I worked at Phillips Publishing, I had a team of marketers working for me. One of the many hats they (and I) wore was writing copy.

As the director of marketing, I was the one to review the supplement copy they wrote for catalog copy, mailings, and inserts. This was long before Google Docs, or even "Track Changes" in Word.

I'd get printouts of their copy drafts, wield my red-ink pen, and the ~~suffering~~ learning would begin.

It wasn't that I took joy in their dejected looks of self-defeat as I handed them their gruesome marked-up drafts bloodied with crits.

I knew I was doing them a favor, and it was what the copy needed for it to work. And we were able to grow that business from zero to $23 million in sales in just three years (that's more than $40 million in today's dollars).

Note: Many of these folks who worked for me and endured the terror of my "red ink pen" went on to have great marketing or copywriting careers and are friends to this day.

But during my time at Phillips Publishing, I also discovered that I needed to be more open and receptive to feedback. On a few occasions while I was there, the entire management team went through Jerry Bell Leadership Training.

This involved having people who reported to you, people you worked with, and people who managed you fill out detailed anonymous questionnaires and provide comments about your strengths and weaknesses (and annoying idiosyncrasies).

Then you'd have an all-day session to learn about the attributes of good leaders, and then—*finally*—get your personal feedback (which for me and many of my colleagues was often hard to hear... especially those sometimes-harsh verbatim comments) handed to you in a large, white sealed envelope.

Before we could tear open the envelope and read its contents, Dr. Bell had each of us take out a blank piece of paper and write on it in big letters:

I LOVE FEEDBACK!

This feedback, which for me and many of my colleagues was often hard to hear, was painful yet transformative. It changed the way I related to my team; it affected how I mentor copywriters today, and even impacted how I parented my two children.

The same is true of all those years when I was an up-and-coming marketer who also wrote copy. I endured the "terror of the red ink pen," getting back pages of copy I'd sweated over filled with so much red ink, you could barely see the type.

But I would still seek out feedback, painful as it might be, whenever I could. Once I stepped out on my own and started freelancing, I took advantage of every chance I had to get someone to review my copy.

There weren't hordes of people back then offering up training or coaching. It was rare indeed to be able to get an in-demand copywriter to give you the time of day.

On a few occasions, conferences I signed up to attend offered a free private copy critique with a top copywriter. I took full advantage!

Sometimes more experienced copywriters who I met at conferences would offer to look at my copy. I took them up on it! (And I always sent them a nice "thank you" gift in return.)

Seek out copy critiques—but be careful out there

One time, I attended a conference in New York City for newsletter marketers. Prior to the conference, I had read about an opportunity to submit a promo to be critiqued by a panel of expert copywriters on stage.

I figured this would be a good opportunity to get some exposure. So I submitted my brand-new financial newsletter control promo... which had just beat Jim Rutz's control.

I thought it would make me look good! But I was wrong...

The three "expert" copywriters (I won't name names, but you'd recognize some of them) began picking apart headlines and subheads in my hot new control promo, and talking about what they'd do differently.

I was sitting there, just taking it in, but inside my head I was like, "You freakin' idiots! It's working great! IT BEAT JIM RUTZ, for crying out loud!!!"

I went back and read the call for copy submissions later which the conference organizers had sent out, and saw it asked for promos people wanted HELP with. I thought it was more of a "let's look at what's working" kind of thing. So my bad!

In any case, I adopted ZERO of their recommendations, and that promo went on to be a control for three more years... and beat Jim Rutz a second time when the newsletter re-launched with a new editorial team!

So be careful WHO you get feedback from. The same is true for your clients.

Don't be afraid to push back when you know you're right

You want to be open to getting your clients' input. After all, they're closer to their product and market than you are. Some of my biggest wins have been promos that were the result of a close, collaborative relationship with the client.

But don't be an "order taker" and automatically implement changes you feel weaken your copy without pushing back. Don't be a jerk, but DO explain why you did what you did (in a non-defensive way).

Calmly explain any issues you see with what they're proposing, and what you think will work best instead to address their issues.

Sometimes, an ego-driven client who thinks they're a great copywriter (they're one of the biggest "red flags" to watch out for— see Chapter 4) won't budge. In that case, it's best to just give them what they want and move on.

Speaking of which, if you're a copywriter or business owner who writes your own copy, and you don't have someone else reading every new piece of copy you write, you're at a serious disadvantage.

While this is especially true if you're in the beginning stages of your career, it's extremely helpful even if you consider yourself a good copywriter and have written successful copy. Even now I sometimes hire a woman I call my "copy therapist" to read copy I write or chief.

It was also extremely helpful to me years ago on those occasions when I've worked with a copy chief hired by the client, or when the clients themselves were pretty smart about copy.

That's because I would actually get useful and valuable feedback on my copy. And getting that input—and most importantly, being OPEN to it—made a real difference in the success of my promos.

I know it's not always fun. After all, you LOVE your copy, right? You hang onto parts of it that are your "darlings" even though they interrupt the flow or go off on tangents or confuse your reader.

But getting that feedback is essential to ensuring your copy is as strong as possible. If it's for your own business, it also helps you get your product or service (that you hopefully believe in and are passionate about) into as many people's hands as you can.

So get someone who's a good copywriter to read your draft of copy and give you feedback. Or ask your client to review your draft with you.

Instead of being defensive or "fighting" for every word of your copy, ask them to explain what they didn't like.

Then put on your body armor of thick skin. You may need it.

Make this your mantra: "I LOVE FEEDBACK!"

Shortening your slog to the top

You can see why one of the best ways to climb the "copywriting ladder" far faster is to work with a mentor or more experienced copywriter to review your copy and provide feedback. You can also gain this advantage by starting out working in-house.

Like I said earlier, the few occasions I got this kind of feedback early on proved extremely valuable.

If you can find a top copywriter who offers this kind of one-to-one review service, definitely take advantage of it if you've got the cash.

But if it's money you really can't afford to part with, there are other ways to keep improving until you do have the cash to spare.

At a virtual copywriting event "cocktail party" I attended a few years ago, I heard one copywriter say, "I'm thinking of going into debt to work with a high-priced copy mentor for one-on-one mentoring... it'll be worth it, right?"

I let him know I thought it was a bad idea to go into significant debt (I think this guy was looking at $30k+) hoping it's going to pay off.

So to him and the others listening in, I offered up another option to consider...

Find yourself a "copy buddy"!

It worked for two top A-list copywriters—Parris Lampropoulos and David Deutsch—decades ago when they were starting out. They both would review each other's copy and give each other feedback.

They put together a "gentleman's agreement" that neither one would go up against one of the other's controls if given the chance (I suspect they still honor it to this day).

They were both dedicated to studying and improving and getting better at their craft. And they helped accelerate each other's learning curves as well.

And it didn't cost them $30k+. Heck, it cost them nothing!

So think about other copywriters you know who are around your same level, and who are just as dedicated and motivated as you are to keep getting GOOD at copy.

Next time you're at a virtual or live event, or if you join a mastermind or get active in a Facebook copywriting group or paid community like Copy Chief, maybe your perfect "copy buddy" match is waiting for you to discover them!

Breaking into royalty-paying copy

Maybe you've been hearing that few, if any, clients are willing to pay royalties. Yet on many occasions, including in recent years, I've earned more than six figures in royalties in a single year from just ONE promo… in some cases, ones I wrote several years prior!

Not only that, a few summers ago after a few weeks in Italy, where I spent my days sightseeing, drinking Aperol spritzes, and not doing a lick of work—and came home to find a fat sum in royalty checks stuffed into my mailbox and bank account.

So I can tell you royalties are alive and well. The internet has changed nothing. Most of these royalties I've had coming in are from online sales pages with traffic coming from Facebook or emails… though some direct mail promos contribute as well.

If anything, the Internet has created a whole lot more opportunity. Especially if you're just breaking into copywriting. You see, most people don't start off as copywriters doing long-form sales letters for sales pages, direct mail, or video sales letter scripts (VSLs).

They usually work their way up to doing them by writing emails that drive traffic to these sales pages, for example… or creating headline and lead tests.

And while the vast majority of copywriters don't write long-form sales pages, direct mail packages, or video scripts, there are ways you can work in performance-based compensation so you can earn more. Revenue share deals where you earn a percentage of sales generated by your email or other copy are one example.

But many copywriters gravitate towards writing long-form promos since they're the "holy grail" of copywriting… where you can earn mostly passive income in the form of royalties, in addition to higher fees.

(You may need to do occasional tests and updates to keep your control running, and some niches, like health or supplements, are more evergreen than others, like financial—which needs ongoing updates to stay current.)

As any A-lister will tell you, you're not taking the job for that so-called "high" fee, you're taking it for the potential royalties, as that's where you can make 10X the fee (or much more) over time if you get a huge winner.

Like I explained earlier in this chapter, I spent most of my time writing short emails, inserts, catalog copy, renewal efforts, and website copy when I first started out as a freelance copywriter.

It was the result of doing well at these various flat-fee copywriting projects that one client gave me the chance to write a long-form copy promotion for a fee plus royalty.

And to get that royalty-paying gig, I convinced a previous client whose sales letters I had merely edited and reworked that he should test a magalog format.

And that he should let ME write it! Which he did… in part, because I gave him a "steal of a deal" flat fee.

But I got something super-valuable out of it that was worth far more than that relatively low flat fee… a SAMPLE!

And I used that ONE sample to send to that later client, who hired me for three times as much plus royalty potential.

The promo I wrote didn't work the first time around. So after revisiting one of my other original "big ideas" and deciding to test that, I rewrote the majority of the promotion (he paid me an additional two-thirds of the original fee to do so… rewrites aren't free!)

And "holy moly…"

I got my first royalty-paying control!

This highly successful promo went on to mail in different formats for ten full years... and paid me nearly a quarter-million dollars in royalties over that time.

The doors were opened to that opportunity by taking smaller "starter" jobs that paid the bills (and still allowed me to generate a six-figure income to replace the salary of the high-level marketing job I had left to start freelancing).

And there are plenty of these "starter" jobs that can lead you to bigger projects—and earnings.

But there's another path if you don't already have experience writing copy or working as a marketer that you may want to consider. I've mentioned it before.

It certainly gave me a huge edge before I ended up going freelance. And that was to work in-house for a major publisher.

And after that, I used a retainer arrangement as a "bridge" between leaving my job and building up my client roster.

But there are some potential pitfalls you'll want to make sure you avoid with either one of these paths.

While you may have gotten into "free"-lancing because you wanted to be "free"... there's the "good" to consider with these arrangements, as well as the "bad"... and then there's the "ugly."

Turn the page and keep reading, and I'll explain...

Chapter 11

The Good, the Bad, and the Ugly About Retainers, Working In-House, and Going "Exclusive"

H ere's a topic that often comes up in copywriting and mastermind groups I'm in as well as in my mentoring sessions.

It's about when you should consider going "in-house" as a copywriter... doing an ongoing retainer deal... or going "exclusive" versus remaining a freelancer.

These arrangements basically fall into one of the following different scenarios:

1) Becoming an actual, *bona fide* employee (remote or on-site), with a benefits package that often includes health insurance, paid vacation time, 401k (often with some kind of employer matching), and other "perks." In this scenario, the employer pays the employer portion of Medicare and Social Security taxes, withholds federal and state taxes, and issues you a W-2. Think of it as getting "married."

2) Going "exclusive" without becoming an employee, where you are technically a 1099 independent contractor. In this scenario, you're responsible for filing and paying your own taxes (including both the employee and employer portion of Medicare and Social Security), you need to get your own health insurance, and do your own retirement savings plan. This is typically an exclusive arrangement, meaning you're not able to work for other clients. Think of it as "living together."

This next one isn't "in-house" or "exclusive", but can result in a full-time, solo-client work arrangement...

3) Setting up a retainer arrangement, where you agree to do ongoing work on mutually agreed-upon terms, often for a set period of time, either part-time or full-time. In this scenario, you're still basically a freelancer, but you've got a steady stream of income from this particular client. Think of it as "going steady" or "dating around" if you've got a part-time retainer in addition to other clients.

The way I've built and run my freelance copywriting business for more than two decades isn't any of these. I've done a few retainer arrangements with clients (one acted as a "bridge" between leaving my marketing job to go freelance).

But none of them has been anything more than part-time, which always allowed me to bring on new clients and maintain existing client relationships.

Because I had built connections and a reputation for being a good copywriter and marketer when I was at Phillips Publishing, when I left to go freelance, I had a steady stream of referrals coming my way.

I still had to "kiss a lot of frogs" (some clients were less than ideal... but hey, that gave me some great "war stories" and they paid the bills). And I generally went from flat-fee to flat-fee project, but the work was always there.

The only dry spell I ever had happened after I'd been freelancing for one year. I had just wrapped up a client project and realized I didn't have anything booked after that.

I briefly panicked, then relaxed just a bit and decided to savor the break.

Turns out it didn't last long... not even a week. Within a few days, some past clients and referrals had booked my schedule solid again.

After a few years, I wrote a few big (and not-so-big) control promos and began writing almost exclusively long-form copy and collecting royalties along with bigger fees.

I share this perspective because at that point in time, the opportunity for me to build my reputation as a freelance copywriter was huge.

I had a steady flow of clients. I had a solid foundational knowledge of copywriting and direct response marketing.

And I had worked in-house with a "name" company (Phillips was at least three times bigger and better-known than Agora Publishing was at the time, and which is now the industry behemoth).

So with all this going for me, plus the fact that after those first few years, I pared my weekly hours to no more than 20 to 30 tops when I was raising my two children (while still making, as one copywriting training company likes to say, "more than most doctors"), *why would I go in-house?*

How to survive and thrive no matter what arrangement you take on

It could be your situation is different than mine was back then. And times have certainly changed.

Like I've said before, there are more potential clients than ever before. There is also more competition from other copywriters than ever before.

You're competing against copywriters from all over the world for clients here in the US. That often wasn't the case a decade or two ago.

The clients tend to be smaller, entrepreneurial companies, versus the direct response behemoths of a decade or two ago. Many of those behemoths are no longer around, or are a shadow of their former selves.

So there's much more pricing pressure on copywriters in terms of the fees they can charge or whether they can negotiate royalty arrangements.

The case for staying a freelancer versus being "chained" to a client

When you have the talent, experience, and skill set to consistently produce quality copy that gets results for your clients, you'll never want for work.

You can charge higher fees... negotiate royalties and other "win/win" incentive arrangements... and, if it's your dream like it was mine, work less and earn more.

So how do you get really good at writing copy? It's not just learning everything you can from the right people. It's actually DOING it.

This takes us back to the topic at hand: should you take on a full-time gig if you're currently eking it out as a copywriter (or even if you're already successful)?

Let me sum up my advice that I'll get into more in-depth in this chapter:

If you are just starting out in your copywriting career, or have a few years of experience under your belt, having the opportunity to work in-house for a well-run, respected company could be a game-changer.

Here's why:

1. You'll get paid to learn, and in return potentially get one of the best direct response copywriting educations money simply can't buy.

2. You'll instantly gain a network of colleagues who "know somebody" who "knows somebody" so if you ever leave (you will eventually) you'll have a huge edge in transitioning to freelance. You may even get lucky and get a wonderful mentor.
3. If you become an actual real employee vs. a 1099 one, you'll potentially save a ton on insurance and taxes… plus enjoy paid time off and 401k matching from your employer (a.k.a. free money!)

Caveats: Finding the right "well-run, respected" company is tougher than it seems… do your legwork. Talk to people who work there, especially those who *used* to work there.

If you're a contract/1099 employee, make sure they're paying you enough. Generally, you should be making about 50% more compared to what they'd pay someone who is a salaried employee getting full benefits… not to mention those extra taxes you're responsible for when you're self-employed.

Take into account what you need to pay for the employer portion of Medicare and Social Security taxes, health insurance, days you take off sick or for vacation without pay, and all the other employee "perks" you're not getting.

And NEVER sign any piece of paper without knowing exactly what you're signing (i.e. get a lawyer to review it).

Common client and employer traps to look out for and AVOID

A common trap you can fall into is being asked to sign a non-compete contract, which are becoming more popular for lower- and mid-level employees.

These agreements generally benefit the employer only, while limiting your ability to earn an income should you leave or be terminated. (I'll get more into these later!)

You also want to avoid a common trap that seems to be on the rise (whether you do freelance or in-house work): NDA agreements that keep you from showing samples of your work to others.

This is something to avoid whenever possible. You don't want to invest months or years of your life and then have nothing to show for it in terms of getting future clients.

Then there's the seemingly lucrative but often risky "exclusive" retainer arrangements.

If you already have established yourself as a copywriter and have a steady flow of clients you like working with, I'd generally advise against in-house or "all you can eat" buffet-type retainer arrangements with one client.

However, if you get the right, senior-enough opportunity with a fast-growing or well-respected company that's willing to reward you, obviously go for it if you want the "peace of mind" and chance to earn big money.

But all too often, what I find is companies want to have copywriters on staff that they keep "captive"... without offering the benefits and promotion opportunities you'd get if you were an actual employee.

You may find yourself dealing with the constantly shifting copy priorities... changes of direction (or lack of planning) that result in endless rewrites... and other undisciplined practices that would often not occur when using a freelancer...

Trust me, these things can make your life so miserable, that big retainer they're paying you isn't worth it!

(I personally know mid-range and top-level copywriters who've had to walk away from nightmare situations like these... even with respected, fast-growing companies.)

Being a *freelancer* puts you in a much better position to push back against this kind of client BS... or to simply say no to it.

It's why I think these types of exclusive arrangements are best avoided unless you really need the work... or they offer you an exceptional opportunity to earn big money (and even equity). At the very least, do your homework beforehand!

Crucial step for keeping the dreaded "scope creep" at bay

Should you decide to take on a retainer or contractor position, make sure the scope of work is clearly defined.

Otherwise, you could find yourself on an endless treadmill of work demands and frustrations that drain you as much or more than if you were stuck in-house in a dysfunctional company in the worst job ever.

One other thing... think long and hard before taking yourself "off the market" and "living together" or even "getting married" to one client.

I remember knowing other top copywriters when I was earlier in my career who would take on one full-time retainer for several months or a year.

Then when it ended, they'd have to basically start all over from scratch building their client base. I know, because they would often call me looking for overflow work.

Once again, it's another reminder why the legendary Dan Kennedy says, "The most dangerous number in business is ONE."

That's why you want to go into any kind of full-time gig arrangement with your eyes wide open... and decide if it's the right opportunity for where you are now—and where you want to go.

Using a retainer as a "bridge" to going freelance

My first retainer played a pivotal role in my career. It was a six-month arrangement... and it allowed me to walk away from my

$100,000-a-year marketing job and make the leap into freelance copywriting.

This retainer arrangement took only half my time, but paid me 90% of what I had been making. I then brought on a few other clients and had no problem making 50% more my first year as a freelancer than I did in my previous six-figure job.

But as I built my freelance copywriting business and took on more and more clients, I steered clear of making that big of a commitment to one client.

For one, I wouldn't have wanted to take myself off the market and risk having my client relationships grow cold.

As I mentioned earlier, if you put all your eggs in one basket with one or two clients… and something goes wrong with that relationship or that client's business that's outside your control…

BOOM! There goes 50% or 100% of your income.

Then there's the long, slow crawl back from obscurity as you try to get to where you once were. So there's an upside and a downside to everything.

But like I said earlier, having that first retainer gave me steady "replacement" income right off the bat so I could leave my high-paying job and go freelance.

And having the right retainer arrangement can help act as a bridge for whatever you want to do, too. Just be smart about playing it to your advantage.

What's more, often your *best* prospect for a retainer client is one of your existing clients.

Think about what you want... and go get it!

I once met a copywriter at an event who told me how much he loves drumming.

He loves it so much that he wants to work less and have his own offer, so he's more in control of his life... and has more time for, well, drumming.

He said he spends time playing drums first thing every morning, so he starts off his day doing something he loves. Then he writes copy for the rest of the day.

I really love the idea of doing YOUR stuff, the things that turn you on, or even if it's self-care like getting that workout in or meditating, DONE first thing.

It's giving yourself priority before everything else. And it stirs up your creative juices so they're ready to flow.

But here's what this copywriter was grappling with: what if he cut back on his client work and launched his own offer... and it failed?

"Fear of failure" is a logical fear when it comes to starting your own business. So I told him something I've heard many times from one of my mentors, Brian Kurtz: "You either get a winner or an education" when you try new things or take risks.

However, launching a new business or offer takes a lot more time, energy, and risk than many people have the stomach for. And this guy made it clear that he wanted to keep drumming first thing every morning, but needed to keep money coming in the door.

So I suggested he see if one of his current clients might be a good candidate for a part-time retainer.

That way he'd have a steady income coming in to cover his basic bills, and wouldn't have to spend time courting and bringing in new clients all the time... and could spend that time launching his new offer (or drumming!)

Another event attendee I spoke with at a roundtable I hosted told me he was looking to leave his full-time job to go freelance. He was already moonlighting with some copy gigs on the side.

I gave the same advice to him: see if one of these gigs could be turned into a part-time retainer, with enough income stability so he can leave his job and then start bringing on other clients.

Reminder: If you're leaving a full-time job with benefits, you'll want to figure out your freelance or independent contractor hourly rate based on your current salary, then increase that by roughly 50%. That's the minimum you should be charging clients for your time in a retainer deal.

Check out the going rates, too... but many freelancers don't take into account the value of their health insurance, employer's portion of Social Security/ Medicare, paid vacation and sick leave, and other benefits they find themselves paying for on their own once they become self-employed.

One other important thing. Whenever I've done a retainer, I make sure I get paid by the 1st of the month for the coming month... not at the end of the month after I've done the work.

I like getting cash up front, just like that classic scene in *Good Will Hunting* where Ben Affleck's character gets four stunned venture capitalists to empty their wallets and hand over all their money.

(This is after he spins around in his chair and says, "Re-TAIN-er!!!")

Well... maybe not EXACTLY like that movie scene, but you get the idea!

How working at a J-O-B can speed you to freelance success

I'll be the first to tell you, having that initial in-house experience at Phillips Publishing, one of the direct response giants at the time, gave me invaluable training and experience that greatly accelerated my freelance success.

By the time I left to go freelance, I had worked as a marketer for thirteen years, in direct marketing roles at a major health insurer and then Phillips Publishing... where I launched and ran their Healthy Directions supplement business.

Understanding marketing and working in-house with profit/loss responsibility gave me a huge edge as a copywriter... not to mention all the brilliant people I got to work with in those in-house roles. It was an amazing training ground.

So one way to shortcut your "climb" is to get an in-house role at a direct marketing company, especially one where you can wear several hats OR become a specialist in an in-demand area of copywriting... for example, emails or funnels.

The key is to make sure you learn the strategy behind these marketing efforts, not just how to write copy.

One of my original mentees decided to take an in-house job as a copywriter with a major publisher and stayed there for just over a year.

He now runs his OWN publishing and supplement business. But he never would have done it without putting in his time and getting "paid to learn."

However, he dodged a bullet at the last minute when one of these was thrown at him...

The "golden handcuffs" that can keep you locked up in misery

Some companies want to bring in a top copywriter for an exclusive arrangement.

They want to pay good money, but their copywriting demands are open-ended. Meaning *unlimited*... that's right. Try to pin them down to a set number of deliverables and it's almost impossible.

(Watch out for "buffet-style" retainer arrangements. They can end up like this, too. Be sure to outline what you'll do in exchange for X dollars clearly in writing.)

Based on what I've heard from some folks who've had these arrangements, they can create the same fresh hell you wanted to get away from in the first place when you decided to go freelance... or even worse.

I've mentioned how these arrangements can bring with them the pressure of unrealistic deadlines and the aggravation of constantly shifting plans and schedules.

But there's one thing that can come with an in-house or exclusive arrangement that can turn this into even more of the equivalent of "indentured servitude…"

It's when they ask (or insist) that you sign a non-compete.

Like I mentioned earlier, non-compete agreements are often used for higher-level employees, and sometimes for more mid-level positions. But they're becoming more common for lower-level positions, too.

They basically prevent you from working with a company, either as an employee or consultant/freelancer, that works in a similar industry for a specific period of time.

These agreements may sometimes be offered up in exchange for stock options or a big promotion or when you're first hired. Other times you're told you need to sign it with the implication your job is on the line if you don't.

I advised my former mentee not to sign one when the company he was working for put one in front of him. Even though he did end up signing it, he left and pursued a different niche when launching his own supplement and publishing business.

How I kept myself "free" so I could eventually go freelance

I'll never forget when I was offered the "golden handcuffs" when I was working at Phillips Publishing. I had recently been promoted to

Associate Publisher, working with luminaries like Jay Abraham and Denis Waitley.

I was subsequently invited to a meeting with the company chairman, Tom Phillips, and company president, the late Bob King, in Tom's huge executive office.

It seemed almost surreal. I sat there basking in praise as Tom and Bob raved on and on about what great work I did and how much I had done for the company and how valuable I was to them. I'd give my eyeteeth to have that on video today!

Then one of them slyly brought out a piece of paper and began talking about it as a kind of formality... and that it would guarantee me "stock appreciation rights" as additional bonus compensation.

(After getting a few questions answered about the value and quantity of these SARs, I did some quick math... I am a former math major, after all. And it looked like the current value came out to about $15k. Even back then, it didn't seem like a lot.)

They clearly wanted and expected me to sign the non-compete agreement right then and there. But I thought back to a conversation I'd had recently with my father, who had just been diagnosed with stage 4 prostate cancer.

I was telling him about what a great life the top freelance copywriters we worked with at the company had. How they worked 20 or 30 hours a week... and many of them made upwards of $300k or $500k a year (and sometimes over a million).

I shared with him that I had been writing a lot of copy as part of my job there and it appealed to me. I felt it was something I could do well at.

And even more so, I craved that kind of flexibility and freedom they enjoyed. Because I had just found out that I was a few months pregnant with my first child.

I hadn't let anyone at work know yet, as it was too soon. Of course, my dad knew... and he encouraged me to look into freelance copywriting further.

With all these things going through my head as Tom and Bob looked at me expectantly in that giant executive office, I told them I'd have to think about it.

Displaying the kind of business competence I knew they admired, I said I wanted to have my attorney review everything, just to make sure I fully understood what I was signing.

I didn't actually have an attorney... but my best friend's husband was one, so I got him to walk me through the agreement and explain everything.

I then made my decision: I wasn't going to sign any piece of paper, especially for that amount of compensation. Because I didn't want anything to impinge on my freedom to one day go freelance.

And a year and a half later, after I'd had my first child and come back to work—only to find myself "mommy-tracked"—I finally decided to take the leap to freelance copywriting.

I didn't burn any bridges behind me, and Phillips Publishing (and Healthy Directions) became one of my top clients pretty much out of the gate.

Sadly, my father didn't live long enough to meet my first child... or my second one... or see my freelance career take shape and blossom. I miss him terribly.

But I always feel he is with me, cheering me on.

What's good for businesses CAN be good for copywriters

Having been on both sides of the equation—as a marketing executive at a top direct response company that worked with top talent like Gary Bencivenga and the late Clayton Makepeace—and as a freelance copywriter, it's clear I have strong opinions on this topic.

When it comes to the most competitive, hard-to-do copywriting that's the lifeblood of many businesses (since it's what brings in new customers), companies benefit most from using freelancers.

That way, they're always bringing in fresh eyes and approaches... and tapping into an accumulation of knowledge that freelancers pick up from working with many different clients in different industries or with different products.

But there are lots of reasons why companies want to hire copywriting talent and bring them in-house:

- They want unfettered access to copywriting services at their fingertips
- They want to train and develop copywriters who know their products and market
- They want to bring in top talent and keep them from working for their competitors

… and that's just naming a few reasons.

And there are lots of reasons you might consider going in-house, depending on your situation.

If you're just starting out, there's no better way to get invaluable marketing and copywriting training and connections than to get paid to learn at a top direct marketing company.

If you're worried about having regular income and/or health insurance benefits, a J-O-B may be for you as well.

If you're able to command a million dollars-plus a year like some top A-listers can, there's the guaranteed money angle at the top of the food chain as well.

But if you don't have a fat bank account and can't afford to not work for six months or a year, watch out for those sneaky non-compete agreements—and make sure they don't end up biting you in the butt or setting up any barriers.

And even if you work on retainer or in-house, chances are at some point you'll find yourself freelancing. If you play it right, you'll eventually find yourself becoming in demand.

That's why you'll want to make sure you pay attention to the advice I'm dishing out in the next chapter...

Chapter 12

When You're the "Hot Girl (or Guy) at the Bar"... or Aspire to Be

I once had a mentoring session with a woman who's a rising copywriting and marketing star at a well-known publisher.

She was struggling with a problem that many people don't realize is actually a problem... one that's filled with hidden landmines and can lead to even bigger problems (even though it seems like a good problem to have!)

I call it "when you're the hot girl at the bar..." but it can also apply to guys, of course.

This woman I was talking to had seen her earnings and responsibilities steadily increase and was bringing in some nice royalties, too. That's a result of the impact her copywriting and marketing efforts were having on the company.

So she was starting to get attention from the higher-ups, who wanted to keep her happy. She'd demonstrated she had what it takes to keep growing and contributing to the company's success.

But now the executives at her company were competing against others outside the company who'd taken note of this rising star... even without her reaching out.

That's why she was now stressing out about being "the hot girl at the bar" and wanted to talk with me.

She now had the heads of other, smaller publishing companies in dogged pursuit... while her in-house bosses kept pestering her for what she wanted to keep her happy.

Just like the "hot girl at the bar," she was the one in control... with her pick of attractive options to choose from. (She ended up moving to another company, where she was able to better maximize her career growth and earning potential.)

But as you're about to see, it's essential to handle this newfound success the right way, to avoid creating big problems—and missing out on big opportunities.

4 rules to help you handle being "in demand" the RIGHT way

It's a powerful position to be in, yet all too often we can start to fall into people-pleasing behaviors and say "yes" to the wrong things... or get swept off our feet by aggressive suitors who promise us the sun, moon, and stars.

That's why it brings on a whole new set of challenges when you go from being a striving, up-and-coming employee... or "feast or famine" freelance copywriter... to suddenly becoming "in-demand."

Most of us recall the struggles of starting out and finding those first clients... and keeping that client pipeline flowing. Perhaps you're stuck in this frustrating phase.

You may have thought, *if only* I didn't have to worry about finding clients... ALL my problems would be solved!

But that's not how it goes. It often means you have a whole NEW set of problems and challenges to navigate.

I've seen many copywriters who end up making costly mistakes when the client pipeline goes from a mere trickle to a raging river. So let's review my rules for being the hot girl (or guy) at the bar:

Rule #1: Don't jump too fast. Be wary of people who want to get "married" after the "first date." If they're giving you the bum's rush, you have to wonder why are they so desperate? You need ample time to consider ALL your choices (and as the hot girl you should demand it).

This applies not just to jumping ship from one company to another, but entering into long-term retainer commitments, or going from freelancer to in-house copywriter. Be rigorous in your research and know that there are always "unknowns" that could turn out to be negative, no matter how good things look on the other side.

Rule #2: Don't say "yes" to everything. When freelancers are going from feast or famine mode to becoming the hot girl (or guy) at the bar, it's likely they still have fear and a scarcity mindset driving them. So they end up saying "yes" to everything that comes their way, because they're afraid if they say "no" it will mean "never."

That's not the case. When you can respond with, "I'm booked up until ___ but I have a slot available for your project in ___," you actually look more valuable and desirable to the potential client.

This is "hot girl at the bar" in action. No, I won't dance with you now... maybe later. (Remember, this is what happened when I met my husband for the first time... at a bar!)

Do this and your "stock" goes up in the eyes of the client. PLUS (even more important), instead of stacking multiple projects on top of each other... stressing yourself out beyond belief and causing you to do poorer-quality work (thus quashing any future work with said clients), you can sit back and relax, and often charge MORE... while collecting 50% advances to save a slot in your schedule.

Rule #3: Be choosier. This is the time to start deciding how to best assemble your "portfolio." Decide what your evaluative criteria will be (i.e. get the data to predict the royalty potential... can this be a project that generates $50-100k a year in passive income—or more—if you get a big winner?)

Or maybe what's important to you is focusing on one niche you love writing for (which can often end up making you more valuable, too). Or maybe you don't want to work as much... or you want to take every Friday off... or take the whole summer off.

Or maybe you ONLY want to do long-form, royalty-paying projects... or maybe you want to focus only on email copy and look for revenue share deals.

The thing to remember is, when you're the hot girl (or guy) at the bar, you can afford to be extra choosy!

Rule #4: Determine your current market value. There's definitely the possibility if you're this hot, you could be way undercharging without knowing it (i.e. your salary and other compensation are less than the value you're bringing to the company... or you haven't raised your freelancing fees enough to reflect your increased skill set and successful track record).

So do your research and figure out what your current market value is. (Keep in mind that as inflation goes up, what you're earning should go up, too!)

If you're an in-house employee, look at what other people are making (yes, ask around, but be discreet). Another way to figure this out is to "talk turkey" (i.e. money) with your many outside suitors before you spend too much time with them courting you to find out what they're willing to pony up for someone with your skills.

Or maybe you want more training opportunities, to get paid bonuses or other incentives, or have the company pay for you to join masterminds or attend live events. Don't be shy about asking for these things, hot girl (or guy)!

If you're freelancing, find out what others at your copywriting level are charging for similar projects. Like I've mentioned before, if

118

you're a woman, you might want to automatically add an additional 25-50% to whatever rate you come up with.

Based on my experience, men are MUCH more likely to feel confident about charging more… even if they're less experienced.

Charge enough that you feel a little nervous sending the bid to the client. Because remember, when you don't charge enough, they don't respect you as much.

If you find yourself in this "hot girl (or guy) at the bar" situation, congratulations on all the hard work and investments along the way that it took to get to this point.

Now, besides getting really good at what you do and producing great results, what's one of the most overlooked secrets to becoming that hot girl (or guy) at the bar if you're not already there now?

3 "catbird seat" moves that prove you're WORTHY to clients

Let's talk about what to do as a copywriter to prove yourself worthy to clients.

By "worthy" I mean worth paying more money to… worth hiring again and again… and worth recommending to others.

Obviously, making more moolah, getting a steady stream of work, and being flooded with constant requests from potential clients is every freelancer's dream.

Yet all too often, when starting out and after landing those first few clients, many copywriters "screw the pooch," for lack of a better phrase.

If you learn from their mistakes (even if they're ones you've made yourself), you can put yourself in the catbird seat to profit.

Okay, that's one of my favorite phrases from when I used to write financial promos, but you get what I mean.

So let's take a look at those catbird seat moves that make clients LOVE you, want to pay you more, hire you over and over, and even FIGHT over you (okay, maybe I'm taking it a bit far...)

Catbird seat move #1: Gain their respect by acting like a professional

In every interaction with your client, especially leading up to getting hired, you want to act like a seasoned pro (even if you're not one just yet). Don't be immediately available, but "check your schedule" and "move things around" if need be (even if you have no work). Don't give the impression you're just sitting there twiddling your thumbs, waiting for the phone to ring, or they'll think you're no good.

Also, don't feel pressured to give out a quote over the phone (you will likely underprice yourself)... especially if it's not an immediately straightforward project.

Instead, tell them you'll email a quote later that day or within the next 24 hours. Once the client accepts your quote, invoice for the 50% advance and send over a client agreement (see my advice in Chapter 7).

And never start doing the work until you receive your advance, even if it's a rush job. That's where the rubber meets the road. You'll find out then if it's really a "Go" if they actually *pay you*.

Remember, it's typical for freelancers, even total beginners, to get 50% upfront. If you don't get one, you could end up screwed.

Don't worry that you're going to turn off the client simply by acting like a professional. It will set the tone for the entire project, and they'll respect you more for it.

(Plus, it could save you countless hassles!)

Catbird seat move #2: Stick to the agreed-upon schedule

One of the easiest ways to impress your client is to actually deliver the copy on time.

What a concept! You'd be amazed how often I hear frustrated clients complain about copywriters they hire going off to write the copy, only to seemingly never be heard from again... or turning in drafts that are days, weeks, or even months late.

Your client has a business to run. They need to be able to plan and execute their marketing plans. They've got graphic designers and printers lined up, and need to commit to their schedule far in advance. That's why it's of utmost importance that you deliver your copy on time. Otherwise, instead of being an asset to their business, you become a liability.

While there may be some flexibility for longer-form promos that typically have a more drawn-out schedule, you should still shoot to be on time, and if you ask for more time, keep it to just a few additional days (like over a weekend).

Pro tip: Be sure you negotiate deadlines in advance that are reasonable and workable for you. Always "pad" a little bit, especially if you're newer to writing copy. It will take you longer than you think to get your copy in tip-top shape. Which leads me to this next tactic...

Catbird seat move #3: Turn in copy that's as perfect as possible

You've worked hard and sweated over every detail of your copy. You may be wracked with fear and wondering, is it good enough?

It's good to be concerned. After all, it's your job to make sure your copy is as perfect as possible! So do what you need to do to ensure that's the case.

You'd be amazed how many copywriters turn in sloppy first drafts full of typos, missing words, run-on sentences, and other easily avoided mistakes. And that's not even getting to whether the copy is convincing enough or well-constructed or all the other factors that are essential to good copy.

If possible, have someone you know read it beforehand. Get feedback on it from a copywriter you trust. Have someone who's similar to your target prospect read it.

And definitely get a proofer to read it (especially if you're writing for the US market and English isn't your first language). Do NOT just rely on computer programs to do your proofing for you.

Polish your first draft to perfection as much as possible. Don't leave any of that to the client… it's what they're hiring you for.

Try reading it out loud to yourself. It's the best way to catch any missing words, typos, punctuation errors, long run-on sentences, or other issues in your copy.

What's more, never turn your copy in to the client at the end of a long day of writing. At the very least, sleep on it overnight and then look at it with fresh eyes the next morning.

If you find you're still needing to do a lot of editing or reworking, sleep on it another night before turning it in, or at least take a shower or go for a walk, and then look at it again.

Repeat as necessary (you could get really, really CLEAN in the process) until you can look at your copy and not want to change anything unless it's something minor.

The ultimate "catbird seat" move...

If you do all three of these things for every copy project you work on, you'll prove yourself as a great copywriter who puts in the work and is worth giving another shot to, even if your copy fails the first time.

It's true! When I first got some of my big breaks starting out, on three different occasions, my initial time up at bat with a long-form promo failed to beat the control. (I'll talk more about this and how to handle failure in the next chapter.)

As it turns out, each of those initial clients gave me another chance, probably because I did all the right things to be good to work with.

And good thing they did, because on each of those second tries, I hit it out of the ballpark and got huge, successful controls.

It was through all these catbird seat moves, where I ended up beating some pretty big-name copywriters, that I really was able to prove myself worthy. And I never had to worry much about finding good clients after that.

By continuously putting in the work and investing in yourself to get better at writing copy, you'll get those big wins someday, too.

And it really is the best way to make more moolah, get rehired over and over again, and have a horde of potential clients trying to squeeze into your schedule.

Or to become the hot girl (or guy) at the bar wherever you may be working.

The better you get at copywriting—which is something that's completely under your control, no one else's—the less you'll have to worry about finding good clients.

And the more successes you get under your belt, the more those clients will come to YOU.

If you think you can get away with not doing these catbird seat moves, think again!

It's not just some top-level copywriters who think they can get away with this kind of behavior (news flash: they can't).

Many a rising copywriting star has found themself beginning to believe they can do so, too. And it can come back to bite them.

That's because clients talk. I've heard them gossip about copywriters they say they will never, ever hire again.

You want to be one of the ones they speak about with nothing but glowing terms.

And while writing successful copy is one way in, being great to work with is what will have them coming back to you... even if your first effort bombed (hey, it worked for me!)

When you get to where you're able to start picking and choosing among the many copywriting assignments coming your way, you'll want to follow this next client management secret...

Think of your copywriting business as an investment portfolio

I've often thought of my copywriting clients and the projects I take on in a given year as an investment portfolio.

And you should do the same thing. Here's the approach I take when it comes to putting together my own copywriting project portfolio:

I have my "cash cows"—the ones I know will likely generate a certain amount of income, or there's an expected level of reward versus risk.

And then I throw in some riskier plays now and then, but sparingly.

One thing I wouldn't do as a freelancer is put 100% of my "stock" into one company... no matter how great it was. (Exception: maybe if I had a sweet salary, revenue share or royalties, and a good amount of equity, but it all depends on the opportunity.)

Remember the big Enron flame-out back in the early 2000s? (If you're too young, Google it.) People put all their retirement savings into their company stock... and overnight, it was gone.

But that's just me. Invest your copywriting client portfolio based on your own needs and level of risk tolerance. Just like an investment advisor would say, your results may vary.

So what process have I used to decide which copywriting projects to take on?

Since I generally only work on long-form copy projects with royalty potential, I often screen projects by asking things like how much sales revenue the current control sales page is generating... or how many pieces they're mailing their current magalog control each month or year.

That way I can calculate how much I could make in the coming year in royalties if I were to beat the control or have a successful launch promo.

With long-time clients, I don't need to do this level of screening, since I already consider them my cash cows and their performance trends are known to me.

But let's say you're doing a launch or something that's outside your usual or not as proven, just like you might throw a little gold or crypto into your investment mix.

Sometimes these wild cards pay off big, and sometimes they don't. Just like deals you may enter into like revenue share or royalty-only deals, go in with your eyes wide open that these are more speculative plays with risks involved.

Here are some other ways to think about your copywriting business as you grow it and become more successful...

Decide what you want to earn... and reverse engineer it!

I'm sharing a great tip I learned from Dan Kennedy. This is one I got the privilege of hearing him present at a mastermind I attended years ago.

His tip was this: decide how much you want to make from your copywriting business... then reverse-engineer how to make it happen.

Think about what's the certain money in your business and start there. Add in the uncertain money you can conservatively expect to earn from things like royalties.

Now add it all up. What's the difference between what you want to make and what you expect to make with your current income sources? What are you going to do to make up that shortfall?

A big part of making up that shortfall—aside from charging higher rates—is finding the right clients. Instead of constantly hustling for new clients, you want to seek out clients who are growing and always need more "stuff."

These are the clients who are most likely to become income partners and offer you opportunities for royalties, bonuses, and even equity as they grow... and you're able to grow together.

This not only gives you greater security right now, it gives you greater long-term growth prospects. The kind that goes beyond being the hot girl (or guy) at the bar, to experiencing true career and personal freedom.

And isn't that ultimately what this whole freelance game is all about?

To get to this point, you'll likely experience what feels like a rollercoaster of success and failure along the way. Ask any A-list copywriter—or any successful person for that matter—and they'll tell you they've all experienced "bombs" and failures multiple times.

The key is to learn from it and NOT let it keep you from taking risks. I'll cover this more in the next chapter...

Chapter 13

Bombing with Brilliance: Losing Your Fear of Failure So it Won't Hold You Back

Many copywriters fear the worst if they write a big promotion for a client and it bombs, or doesn't do nearly as well as hoped. And they're not sure how to handle it.

Whether you're a newbie or a grizzled copywriting veteran, it's easy to blame yourself. And sometimes, that's where the blame belongs if you took shortcuts or otherwise didn't put your all into your copy.

But you can end up having your copy bomb even if you do everything right.

One thing that always gave me some perspective on this was when I worked for Phillips Publishing. The company would hire the very best copywriters in the business... many of the names are considered legendary.

Because the company was hiring these writers in hopes of getting a breakthrough promotion, they wanted them to take big (but smart) risks. That's how you get the big winners.

And what that means is, sometimes those big risks will fail... on occasion, spectacularly.

While I was there, I saw that even the best copywriters in the world (ones that are considered legendary today) wrote promos the company paid them as much as $100,000 to write... and they would sometimes BOMB.

But they'd be booked to write that next promo... and the next... and the next... and at least one of those would end up being a huge winner.

Like the president of the publishing division I used to work for would say, "If you're not failing enough, you're not trying enough new things."

It's how you get that *next* breakthrough... that *next* big success.

As a result, going into freelance copywriting, I knew that some of the very best copywriters would sometimes fail.

This gave me a certain confidence... a way of looking at things whenever I wrote something that didn't work.

And I managed to make some of my initial "bombs" some of my most successful promos by going back and looking at what I'd learned, then taking a different approach.

The best clients won't ghost you or refuse to hire you again if your copy doesn't initially work for them. Instead, they'll work with you so you can turn your failures into big winners... or, at least, valuable lessons.

It all depends on your arrangement with your client and your desired ongoing relationship. If it's a complete bomb, it doesn't just affect your client; it affects you, too.

That's especially true if you've got a potential royalty or bonus on the line. Then your promo may need some rewriting to have a shot at becoming a winner.

One way to know if even that kind of major surgery is going to work is whether it's been successfully sold via that sales channel before via a previous promotion.

Otherwise, you don't really know if it's bombing because of the copy (and/or the design, which can also make a significant difference), or due to something else.

The "something else" could include everything from not being a product the market desires, having a bad offer (i.e. too high a price or not enough urgency), or not sending it to the right lists.

Let the 40/40/20 rule free you from shouldering all the blame

As copywriters, we need to remember that while in the most competitive niches, copy can be a huge needle-mover, it's not 100% responsible for the success or failure of an ad or promo.

Far from it...

Perhaps you've heard of the "40-40-20" rule of direct marketing. Adapted from the Mad Men advertising era of the 1960s and credited as the brainchild of marketer Ed Mayer, it helps explain the reason for the success or failure of any promotion.

Basically, it's 40% list (or audience) that the ad is going to... 40% offer (meaning the product that's being sold and at what price, including any bonuses, etc.)... and just 20% creative (meaning copy AND design, format, etc.) So, as you can see, your sales copy generally is responsible for less than one-fifth of the success.

Yet all too often, clients want to blame it all on the copywriter. And we put our tails between our legs and slink away.

Obviously, you don't want to do this. It's why you want to work with your client to see how you can potentially give your copy another shot.

Often, it's worth doing so, but you have to do some analysis first and see what insights it leads you to.

Keep in mind that typically your copywriting fee is for one version only. So if your copy needs a lot of reworking, figure out how to price the extra work… or decide if it's a manageable amount that's worth doing at no extra charge to get yourself another shot at a winner.

Chances are if your promo came within 15-20% of beating the existing control, it might just need a new main headline and lead at the beginning of the promo. This shouldn't take you much time, since you're already done all the research and other legwork.

In that case, I'd recommend coming up with some new headlines and leads at no additional charge in the hopes they'll give your promotion another chance with a re-test (particularly if you have a potential royalty on the line!)

Learn what you can and then put it in your rear-view mirror

Regardless, it's important to go back and see what you can learn from any failure. Then make sure you put it in your rear-view mirror and move forward.

Keep in mind the following lessons I've learned from failing on multiple occasions then ultimately succeeding…

Lesson #1: Failing does not mean you suck.

If you bomb out the first time you get your big break, it's not the end of the world.

Three of my first big promo opportunities when I was starting out ended up not working, or even bombing, when they were initially tested.

I took the opportunity to learn from these failures, work with my clients to retest them (often getting paid a whole new fee if it was a complete reworking needed), and ended up with some of my most successful controls.

One of these initial failures I turned into a promo that went on to beat the late, legendary Jim Rutz… not just once, but *twice*.

Another one of these initial failures I changed the headline and lead on and got a big fat control for Boardroom, a top publisher who was a major mailer... making me the first female copywriter to do so! To achieve this, I had to beat a seven-year "unbeatable" control written by superstar A-lister Parris Lampropoulus.

And for the third initial failure, I did a complete reworking and repositioning on a joint supplement promo. It ended up mailing in different versions as a control for more than ten years!

All these initial failures I turned into successes, along with long-running client relationships, and a steady stream of hundreds of thousands of dollars in royalties.

Remember, when I had these first few initial failures I shared, I was far from being considered an A-list copywriter. I wasn't really on anyone's radar. I was basically still a nobody.

But what I learned was this: those clients you have your initial failures with can end up becoming some of your best clients.

That's why you should always put forth your best effort and be good to work with (meet deadlines, communicate, don't whine or argue when you get feedback... you know, the basics I covered in the last chapter).

It's also important to remember this next lesson...

Lesson #2: If you fail, the client is at least partly responsible.

I say this having once been a marketing director and publisher on the client side for Phillips Publishing who worked with a wide range of copywriters, including top A-listers.

Most direct marketing professionals get that no one bats 1,000 when it comes to writing successful promos... they expect some tests will fail. It's the way it works.

So if your client doesn't get it and blames you 100% for something that failed, they're failing to take responsibility for their part. After all, they approved and tested your copy, and chances are, based on the 40-40-20 rule, the real issue isn't just copy.

They may have a terrible offer or guarantee, they may be going to terrible lists, or they may have a terrible product no one wants. There's a whole host of potential issues.

Yet in spite of all this, often the copy—and the copywriter—gets 100% of the blame! You don't deserve that. And it's yet another reason to choose your clients wisely.

Especially when you get a client who wants you to do this next thing...

Lesson #3: If your promo fails, the client does not get "free rewrites" till the end of time (or a penny of their money back).

There's no way you—or anyone else—can guarantee results. There are just too many variables that are beyond your control that affect how your promo performs. Hopefully, you've been crystal clear in your proposals and contracts with your client in order to manage expectations.

You've clearly stated what the "kill fee" will be if the project is cancelled at each stage of the project.

(For example, if the client cancels or "kills" the project after you've already handed in your first full draft, your 50% advance serves as the kill fee... or you can say they owe you an additional 25% at this point. Typically, after the second full draft is done, your kill fee should be 100%, meaning they still need to pay you the remaining 50% balance.)

You've clarified the number of rounds of edits.

(If it's a flat-fee project, generally you'll say your fee allows for up to two rounds of changes before needing to charge a pre-stated amount per hour for the time it takes to make additional changes. If it's a project with royalty potential, you'll generally do as many of rounds of changes as needed without charging extra.)

You've unequivocally stated in your invoice and contract that any advance paid is non-refundable.

(Important! Especially for certain types of clients I've already warned you about.)

But what if you didn't cover your butt properly before you began working with a client… and things start to go awry? It's important to stay professional, try to work with the client to resolve things as reasonably as possible… and stand up for yourself in the process.

Like I've said before, any client who expects free rewrites until you get a winner is being unreasonable, unless they're paying you a much larger fee than usual that spells out this requirement in advance. So if your client wants a significant revamping of the copy you wrote—beyond a simple headline and lead or offer test—they should expect to pay you an additional fee.

Exception #1: When you should ALWAYS make free updates

I always make free updates (if they're not significant—no more than a few paragraphs) or provide a new headline and lead to test, email ads to drive traffic, or other tests when I have a current control that I want to keep alive and generating royalties for me.

But if a huge chunk of the promo needs to be changed—sometimes simply because the product has changed or there's a new spokesperson, that's getting into rewrite territory and an additional fee may apply, depending on the amount of rewriting needed.

Exception #2: When you should ALWAYS agree to a free re-test

If your initial test didn't beat the control but performed respectably, or came close to winning, see if you can do a re-test or re-working of the promo.

Again, don't offer to do a complete do-over for free, unless you really need that sample. But if it's just trying a different headline, lead, or offer, do it for free if they're willing to give you another shot.

I hope these lessons give you some new and valuable insights into running your copywriting or freelance business.

You deserve to be treated as the professional you are. And I get upset when I see other copywriters getting used and abused by clients... or bending over backwards to yield to their unreasonable demands.

Not only is it bad for them, it's bad for all of us, as it rewards bad client behavior and makes them think their expectations are reasonable.

So they try them on the next hungry copywriter that comes along, too. We let enough of them get away with it, and it becomes an industry norm.

Consider this book my way of wisening you up so you won't become their next victim.

Doing this next thing will help make it even easier to develop the thick skin needed to keep your confidence strong and imposter syndrome at bay...

Develop the guts of steel you need to thrive as a copywriter

Just like you may develop buns of steel when you work out regularly, you need to develop guts of steel if you want to succeed as a copywriter... or really, at any challenging endeavor you take on.

I'm talking about being able to stomach failure, rejection, and all the other things that come with freelancing.

That's how you learn to succeed spectacularly: by failing spectacularly. And learning from it.

It's also the key to banishing imposter syndrome and feeling confident... even when you're not. (I'll talk about this more in the next chapter.)

Think about the negative self-talk that's on an endless loop in your brain that keeps you from getting started writing copy. Well, what's feeding into that endless loop?

Each and every "your copy didn't work" email you get from a client... each time a client ghosts you... every time you get back a draft with more track changes edits than actual copy...

Every one of those cold outreach messages you sweated over that languish in inboxes going ignored... and all the other imposter syndrome-confirming things that come with being a freelance copywriter.

But you know what? You've done something most people don't do.

You've put yourself out there! That alone takes guts.

And if you've been in this copywriting game a while, like I have, you've already started to develop those guts of steel.

You HAVE to. It's either that or crawl under a rock.

Here's another surprising thing about failure...

Sometimes you *need* to fail to give yourself that push to succeed

Nothing will teach you more about mental toughness and resilience than having to go through hard things and find yourself coming out on the other side.

It's about failing over and over... and getting back up each time. Everyone does this when they learn to do new things.

Think about when you first learned to ride a bike. You fell at least a few times. And you got up and hopped back in the saddle again. That's how you learned.

That's why you sometimes *need* to fail to give yourself that push to do better.

I remember working as a part-time telemarketer for a waterproofing company one summer while I was in college (this was besides two other part-time jobs I held).

On the first day, I was handed a list of numbers to call, a pre-written pitch offering a free basement inspection, and told I needed to get at least three leads a day.

Sounded easy enough. But the first two days, despite adhering to the pitch, I got zero leads (and more hang-ups, cussing, and rejections than I can count).

On the third day when I came to work, the call center manager pulled me into her office as soon as I walked in the door. She sternly told me if I didn't get at least three leads that day, I'd be fired.

Now, I needed this summer job in order to help cover my college expenses that my student loans didn't. So I gave it my all that day... and tried tweaking the script, adapting it to each prospect I talked to (looking back, it was a great intro to copywriting).

I got three leads that day, and continued to meet or exceed my lead quota every day after that. Would I have done as well if I didn't fail initially? Probably not.

It's the same thing when it comes to writing copy. It's all about learning and getting pushed to do better.

You may have to be the one to give yourself that push. But when life forces you to do so, it's amazing how effective a motivator it can be!

So find someone or something (a mentor, a fellow copywriter, or your own inner critic) to PUSH you to commit to constant improvement... no matter how good a copywriter you are now.

Because those who get too comfortable are often headed for a fall without realizing it, since the motivation to keep doing your best can start to wane over time. If you're smart, you'll prevent those wake-up calls before they happen... and learn everything you can from them when they do.

Get practice doing things you find scary

The same is true for dealing with rejection. I was reading the other day how the famous philosopher Diogenes the Cynic was once seen begging for money from a statue. When asked what he was doing, Diogenes replied, "I'm getting practice in being refused."

When we don't have experience doing scary things like approaching potential clients or speaking on stage or asking for a raise or fee increase, we tend to avoid doing them. Perhaps we've had a whiff of what it's like to be turned down or blown off, and we don't want to experience it again.

But it makes us too conservative, unwilling to take risks, and leaves us struggling, unable to reach our financial goals or get a shot at potential opportunities. It's not a good way to live.

The more practice you can get doing hard things... and surviving the rejections and failures that follow... the more resilient—and confident—you'll get.

I remember back when I couldn't get my dream prospects to even respond to my cold outreach emails, or felt like I was getting brushed-off when I approached them at conferences when I was first starting out.

Then, a few years later, after finally getting a few big winners under my belt (after bombing several times), they came looking for ME.

Hopefully, these mindset lessons I've shared on "failing your way to success" have helped ignite some new thinking and perspective... and will keep you moving forward in the face of failure and rejection.

And any failures you have? As I mentioned before, learn all you can from them.

Then make yourself able to selectively forget the bad feelings you experienced.

I suppose it's part of building resilience: not constantly ruminating on things that don't work out or the painful things that you've had to endure.

Those failures, bombs, mistakes, insults, or whatever else has you feeling down on yourself... and that happen to ALL of us because we're human...

They don't define you.

So put it in your rearview mirror... hit the gas... and let's head off to the next wonderful challenge or adventure life throws at us.

Because that's what we do. And it's all good.

Chapter 14

How to Banish "Imposter Syndrome" and Act Confident... Even When You're Not

This final client badassery secret I'm going to illustrate with a story from my college days at Miami University. (It's in Ohio, dammit! That used to be a saying on t-shirts due to the many mix-ups with that *other* university that happens to be in Florida.)

We'll call this story...

Two drunk sorority sisters walk into a bar

It was a Saturday night in Oxford, Ohio. One of my sorority sisters and I made our way uptown in this hopping college town after hitting a few parties.

The line to get into one of our favorite bars, The Balcony, was way too long. So we went around the building and climbed up the rear stairs, entering the upstairs bar from the back, where the pool tables were. There were three or four tables, all with guys swigging beers and smoking cigarettes while they played pool.

I asked my friend Gail, "Wanna play?" She was like, "I'm no good."

I told her not to worry.

139

Client Badassery Secrets

You see, back in my youthful preteen days, I'd learned from an old guy named Leo—who lived in the Florida condo complex I lived in briefly growing up—how to shoot pool.

I hadn't really kept up with it in college, but I thought I could still play okay.

So I went up to one of the pool tables where two guys were playing, plunked down a few quarters, and said, "Winner."

They both looked at me, half-smiles on their faces. Like they were thinking, "Yeah, right... she'll be easy to beat."

And to be honest, I'd had at least a few beers. Not drunk, but definitely a bit buzzed.

They finished their game, and I suggested Gail and I play doubles against both of them.

Since they had the table, one of the guys shot first. He did the break, but nothing went in.

It was my turn next. First shot: solid into one of the side pockets. Okay, so we were solids.

Gail and I giddily high-fived each other while the guys shrugged and looked on.

Then I shot another solid, and it landed in the corner pocket. And another. And another. And another.

By this time, the guys had gotten pretty quiet as they watched me closely.

It was still my turn. I'd gotten all the solids in, one right after the other. Now it was time to call the pocket for the 8-ball.

I long-shotted it exactly where I wanted it to go.

Boom! The 8-ball goes into the pocket I called.

GAME OVER.

Let's just say the guys were a bit stunned. I don't think they expected this young, slightly inebriated sorority girl was going to run the table.

Don't let people underestimate you

I can't tell you how many times people I looked up to and respected tried to talk me out of being a copywriter.

I'd hear how "hard" it was, how "no one gets any good until they're in their 40s or 50s," and other such nonsense.

I always had to rely on my own inner belief in myself to take the leap and keep trying, even after failing a few times with major dream clients.

But, while resilience is important, there's one other top trait that every copywriter needs: *confidence.*

You need *confidence* so when you meet a potential client in person at an event, and you're getting vibes like they think you're some newbie or desperate for work, you can project that quiet confidence.

You need confidence so even when you haven't done a particular type of project before, you believe in your own ability to do whatever is needed to figure it out.

You need confidence so when it comes time to negotiate with a potential client, you can ask for what you're worth and push back if they make requests that aren't reasonable.

When they size you up with a glance, assume you're not someone to reckon with, and try to make you feel small... like that doubting glance those pool players threw my way when I plunked down my quarters...

PROVE 'em wrong!

Beating imposter syndrome so you can prove 'em wrong

There's one thing that can really bring down your confidence…

It's imposter syndrome. Even top copywriters deal with it.

You likely have a lot more going for yourself than you may think. It's often difficult, if not impossible, to see yourself as others see you.

But remind yourself just how awesome you are whenever possible (positive self-talk really works). We often focus on our own shortcomings and weaknesses way too much, and ignore our own strengths and accomplishments.

So maybe update that resume. Put together that website. And ask past clients, bosses, and co-workers to write a testimonial for you.

Then luxuriate in that feedback, those accomplishments, that personal story that's yours and yours alone. Let it build you up. Start to BELIEVE it about yourself.

Play the role of consultant and advisor to your clients (who often know far less about direct response copywriting than you do, unless they're one of the big publishers or supplement companies) versus being an order taker.

Put in place those golden rules I shared with you earlier for running your freelance copywriting business like a badass.

Set those boundaries… and say no to clients from hell or who won't work on your terms—including paying you what you're worth.

All these things will help boost your confidence and help you overcome imposter syndrome.

Clearing out the mental garbage that's holding you back is crucial if you want to find your happy place in this crazy copywriting and direct marketing business… and in life.

Because once you get better at setting boundaries... banishing imposter syndrome... taking risks and learning from failure... and using feedback to improve your skill set and deliver better results...

The sky truly is the limit!

Remember... you are a magician (and much more)!

After everything I've taught you so far... all the proven tactics and strategies I've personally used and shown others how to apply successfully...

There's really just one thing that could be either helping you soar or holding you back.

It's your *confidence*.

I want you to know and feel confident that you can DO this!

Think about this...

You are a magician.

You type words on a keyboard... and make money appear out of thin air.

You are a warrior.

You fearlessly take the road others are afraid to take, and soldier on in victory as well as defeat. (It's okay, you can take it and bounce back even stronger.)

You are a mind reader.

You are able to make complete strangers think you know them inside out. You describe their greatest hopes, wishes, dreams, and fears in the same language inside their heads.

You are a professional.

You've invested time and money into building your skill set, and are worthy of the respect you've earned. Don't let anyone ever make you think otherwise.

You are worth it.

Don't be afraid to ask for what's fair, for what you deserve. Know the value you bring to the table.

I hope these *Client Badassery Secrets* help show you the way.

Yours for smarter marketing,

Kim

Wrap-Up: Putting Your Newfound Client Badassery to Work

Where do you go from here?

Where do you go from here, now that you know about the 7 types of clients you meet on the road to copywriting hell... the ins and outs of nicheing... my three golden rules for running a lucrative, hassle-free freelance business... how to lose your fear of failure and banish imposter syndrome... and the best ways to leverage the power of referrals?

Where do you go now that you've heard some of my best (and worst) freelancing war stories... gleaned new insights on finding good clients, leveraging referrals, going in-house or exclusive, negotiating better-paying deals, and raising your rates (you're likely long overdue)... and knowing what to do when you're the hot girl (or guy) at the bar?

Where do you go now that you've hopefully gotten a bit of a confidence boost... an instant wisening up about the good, the bad, and the ugly when it comes to freelance copywriting... and a burst of motivation to make whatever changes you need to make now to ensure you earn more, gain greater flexibility and respect, and build the thriving freelance business you want and deserve?

I've got a few ideas, of course.

First off, if you're not already on my *Copy Insiders* email list, get yourself on it pronto!

That way you'll get my popular *Copy Insiders* e-letter when it's hot off the "press"... my insight-packed "What's in Kim's Mailbox" promo breakdowns... and my marketing emails when I promote my own courses and trainings, along with others whose quality offerings I want to make available.

(Many people love reading and analyzing my sales emails as much as they do my content-packed ones. We copywriters are a weird bunch—but hey, why not geek out on good copy?)

To join my list and get my immensely valuable *Ultimate A-List Copywriter's Promo Checklist*, which is really five different checklists in one, go to **www.KimSchwalm.com**.

While you're there, be sure to check out my courses and trainings—an important step in upgrading your copy skills and becoming an in-demand copywriter. Plus, you can read my blog and catch up on some of what you've missed by not being a Copy Insider!

Second, go to: **toolkit.clientbadasserysecrets.com** to claim your FREE *Client Badassery Tool Kit*. It's your free thank-you gift from me for reading this book.

In it, you'll find two invaluable tools: my *Client Badassery Secrets Client Screening Questionnaire* to help you weed out lousy clients before you take them on... and my *Client Badassery Secrets Sales Call Script* to help you close the good ones AND negotiate better-paying deals!

Third, be sure to spread the word if you got a lot of value out of this book. Send your friends and colleagues to Amazon.com to buy their own copy. And once they do, make sure they claim their own *Client Badassery Secrets Tool Kit*, too!

Fourth, make sure you leave a review so others who need this book will be motivated to get it into their hot little hands. You can post your review on Amazon ☆☆☆☆☆ and I'll be forever grateful.

Now you're ready to go out there… chase your dreams… and build the freelance copywriting business—and life—you want. You can do this.

Drop me a line at Kim@kimschwalm.com anytime and let me know how it goes!

Acknowledgments

There are so many people to thank, I don't know where to begin.

My career as a copywriter would never have happened had I not been hired at Phillips Publishing to help create and market products to subscribers of their newly launched and fast-growing newsletter, *Health & Healing*.

So I have the team at Phillips who launched that newsletter—including my friend and top copywriter, Carline Anglade-Cole, a marketer on the team—along with the late great copywriter, Clayton Makepeace, for helping to create that job opportunity for me. I also want to thank Julie Noble for hiring me and being a fantastic boss and mentor… along with the late Bob King, from whom I learned many invaluable marketing lessons.

Everything else in my career really took off from there: helping to launch and run the Healthy Directions supplement business… gaining skills and experience with copywriting, and the direct marketing strategy behind it… and ultimately going freelance, with Phillips and Healthy Directions as initial clients.

I'd like to thank all those former colleagues who referred me to other clients when I was starting out as a freelance copywriter. I'd like to thank Rick Popowitz for offering me a retainer arrangement that acted as a bridge between my career at Phillips and going freelance, which allowed me to make the leap. I'd like to thank my good friend Belinda Brewster, who went freelance a few years after I did and with whom I shared many a nightmare client story (and even experienced some of them together).

I'd like to thank Ben Settle for giving me the nudge to start sharing and teaching my copywriting knowledge, build a list, and for being a great business partner when promoting my courses to his audience. I'm also thankful he put me in touch with so many incredible entrepreneurial women who I'm grateful to know, and whose support and friendship I cherish to this day.

I'd like to especially thank my husband of nearly 30 years, Bruce, for always supporting my career... for saying, "Yes, you should go to that conference... I'll handle the kids." For pointing out opportunities that I sometimes had blinders to. For listening to the griping, handling all my technology needs, picking up dinner, pouring the perfect wine to go with it after a particularly stressful day, and always cheering me on.

I'd like to thank my two children, Victor and Olivia, who gave me the "why" to walk away from my six-figure marketing job in 1998... and pursue a freelance copywriting career that would give me greater control, more freedom and flexibility, and the career satisfaction and high earning potential I was seeking. You gave me the motivation to fit my work day between your school hours, turn away clients, and focus on a smaller range of projects—which ultimately allowed me to produce better work and earn more. I loved being able to do all the mom things with you and see you grow up into the wonderful young adults you are now. I feel like between you, your dad, and my freelance career, I had it all.

I'd like to thank my mini-goldendoodle Pearl, who passed away while I was writing this book at the age of fourteen-and-a-half. She was who I snuggled with on those days I stepped away from my desk to write headline ideas or fascinations on a pad of paper... who had a dog bed in my office where she'd sleep while I worked... and who got me out on frequent walks in the woods, where I'd often get some of my best ideas (and who would run with me back to the house before I forgot them!) I miss you, my dear pooch.

I'd like to thank my parents, since without them, of course, none of this would be possible. My father passed away when I was pregnant with my first child, and I was still working at Phillips Publishing. I had talked with him about the freelance copywriters we worked with, and how I envied their flexibility and earnings. He was the first to encourage me to think about going freelance. I'm glad I listened. I only wish he had lived long enough to meet my son (and daughter who came later).

I'd also like to thank my mother for being an incredible storyteller, a trait she inherited from her father, and hopefully I've gotten just a smidgen of that trait as well. She also demonstrated the art of negotiating on many occasions, teaching me many valuable lessons. (I'll never forget how she wheeled and dealed on my first car—a go-cart I paid for myself with my babysitting earnings when I was twelve years old.)

I love that when I moved my mom out of her condo last year, I found she had saved several direct mail promos I had written that she got in the mail. I love that she is proud of what I've done and even though she doesn't understand everything I do, she loves that she raised a badass woman, following her lead and a long line of grandmothers and great-grandmothers before her. If anyone taught me how to stand up for myself, it was my dear mom.

Last but not least, I want to thank everyone who helped me make this book a reality. First and foremost, Vicky Quinn Fraser of Moxie Books, whose MicroBook Magic program gave me the support, tools, and framework to get this book done. Theresa Waggott, who provided valuable insights and editing, along with marketing support. And Laura Valenti, who designed the covers and is a delight to work with.

Then there are my beta readers who I want to sincerely thank, all of them Copy Insiders, who dove into my first full draft and gave me amazingly helpful feedback: Sammy Musgrave, Michael Low, Annu Sharma, Damilola Michael, and Mike Garner (a published author whose own book I recommend).

I would like to thank Sammy in particular for her initial feedback after getting my earlier ebook. The immense confidence boost and motivation it gave her almost immediately that she wrote me about is what made me decide to write this book and make it available to as many people as possible.

To all of you... THANK YOU!

About the Queen of Client Badassery... Kim Krause Schwalm

KIM KRAUSE SCHWALM was always a marketer who could write copy.

She spent more than thirteen years in the corporate world in various marketing positions—from marketing director to brand manager to publisher.

Kim also helped launch and run the Healthy Directions nutritional supplement business—and grow it to the equivalent of more than $40 million in sales in today's dollars within its first three years.

Now, more than two decades later, she's built a reputation as one of the top A-level direct response copywriters in the country. She's developed a proven track record of writing successful copy for a wide range of respected publishers, leading supplement businesses and other companies, as well as *New York Times* best-selling authors.

Kim is also the founder of the Get Dangerously Good copywriting training and mentorship hub. It's where she helps copywriters become dangerously good at their craft—and master the techniques, client management skills, and CEO mindset that will make them A-list exceptional in their industry.

Plus, she's spoken on stage at top-tier conferences like The Copywriter Club In Real Life (TCC IRL), Copy Chief Live, Copy Accelerator, and AWAI's Copywriting Bootcamp.

Kim holds a Bachelor of Science in Mathematics and Statistics from Miami University, and earned her MBA in Marketing from Loyola University. She credits her creative and analytical mind and marketing know-how for giving her a must-needed edge in today's increasingly competitive copywriting world—and wants to help others gain the same marketing-savvy advantage.

Kim is one of the few top copywriters who still writes copy for select clients, while also sharing her knowledge with others. Along the way, she's mentored dozens of copywriters and business owners, including some of today's hottest rising superstars.

You can learn more about Kim's copywriting training programs and read her blog at www.KimSchwalm.com. You'll want to get your hands on her *Ultimate A-List Copywriter's Promo Checklist*, yours free when you join her list (and get the *Copy Insiders* emails everyone raves about)!

Made in the USA
Monee, IL
28 March 2025

14771521R00114